The STAGE LIGHTING HANDBOOK

The STAGE LIGHTING HANDBOOK

FRANCIS REID · FOURTH EDITION

A & C BLACK · LONDON
THEATRE ARTS BOOKS/ROUTLEDGE · NEW YORK

Fourth edition 1992
A & C Black (Publishers) Limited
35 Bedford Row, London WC1R 4JH

ISBN 0-7136-3439-1

© 1992, 1976, 1982, 1987

First edition 1976 published by Pitman Publishing Ltd
Second edition 1982 published by A & C Black (Publishers) Ltd
Third edition 1987 published by A & C Black (Publishers) Ltd

Published simultaneously in U.S.A. by
Theatre Arts Books/Routledge
29 West 35th Street, New York, NY 10001

ISBN 0-87830-013-9

CIP catalogue records for this book are available from the British Library and
the Library of Congress

Typeset by ABM Typographics Ltd, Hull
Printed and bound in Great Britain by The Bath Press

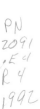

Contents

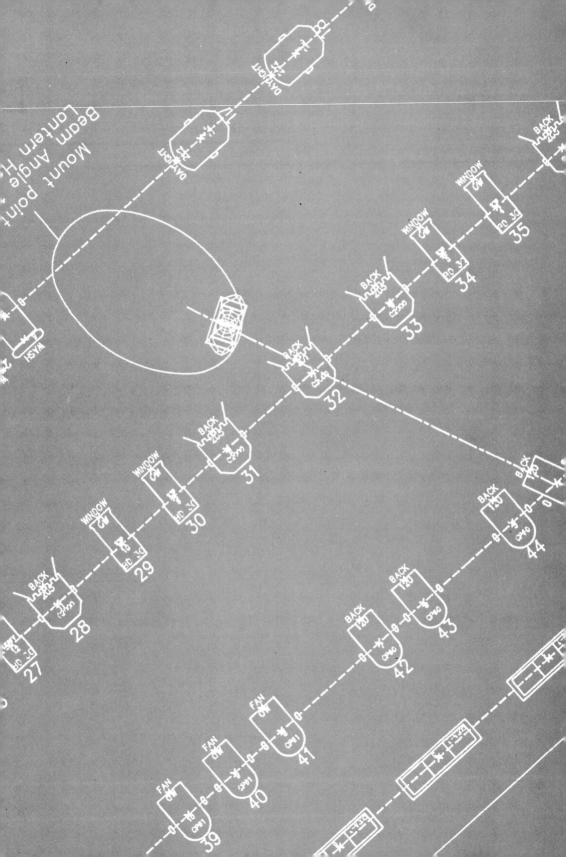

Prologue

It is easy to be poetic about light in the theatre, and a great deal of lip service is paid to its possibilities. Certainly, lighting techniques have shown a tremendous development in the last two or three decades, and there are now a large number of lighting specialists. But no theatre, whether it be amateur or professional, can thrive on over-specialisation.

To twist an old phrase, every theatre person must be a 'Jack of all trades and a master of one'.

A jack of all trades should not dabble in electricity but every theatre person should know something about light. Therefore, this is not a book about electricity: it is a book about light.

If light is an actor's environment, then every actor should have a basic understanding of light in the theatre, should think about how the production is trying to use light, and how that light can help to project script and actor to the audience. Every designer, whether of scenery, costumes, or properties, should be able to visualise the finished product under stage lighting conditions.

But theories about the Art of lighting are useless without some knowledge of the Craft: the way in which the desirable becomes the possible. Every user of light, every director, every designer, every actor, should have some knowledge of what is technically possible – not in terms of electricity, but in terms of light.

In theatre, there is no positive, clear-cut, *good* or *bad*, *right* or *wrong*. It is a very subjective art – who, for example, shall be bold enough to define a good actor? The lighting designer, in the midst of rehearsal pressures, might be tempted to equate good acting with the ability to find light. Hardly a universal definition of good acting!

This book cannot, and does not, set out to lay down objective standards for good lighting. It merely discusses some of the possibilities of light and how these can be turned into reality under practical stage conditions.

In the sixteen years since the first edition there have been considerable developments in lighting instruments, colour filters and control systems. But the basic facts of lighting do not change. The underlying philosophy remains the same: *it ain't what you put, it's the where that you put it.* Improvements in the tools of the lighting design trade do not automatically lead to improvements in the quality of the lighting design. Efficient robust spotlights and sophisticated micro-processor controls may speed up the lighting process. They may reduce or even eliminate some of the old problems so that the lighting designer is free to concentrate on visual ends rather than technical means. But unless the right type of lighting instrument, with the right colour filter, is hung in the right position and pointed at the right part of the stage, any expenditure on the latest marvellous modern equipment will be in vain.

Consequently, while the equipment chapters in subsequent editions have been amended to take account of new developments, the chapters dealing with the principles of lighting design and lighting management have been expanded and hopefully clarified.

The author, in his continued attempts to find ways of expressing a visual medium in words, has been helped by his colleagues in the professional theatre and by the many students with whom he has explored lighting's contribution to the performance environment. To all his students at the the Central School of Art and Design, the Royal Academy of Dramatic Art, the National Theatre School of Canada and in many parts of the world (particularly Australia, India, New Zealand, Singapore, Spain and Sweden) he once again offers his sincere thanks for the continuing way in which they have sharpened his wits by asking searching questions.

For the illustrations, the author is indebted to Strand Lighting and their magazine TABS, the technical theatre review CUE, Arri, Avolites, CCT, DHA, Le Maitre, Lightworks, M & M Lighting, Modelbox, Optikinetics, Ludwig Pani, Rosco, Teatro, Thomas Engineering, Vari-Lite, White Light, W. G. Crisp, James Twynam, and Barrie West.

1
Aims in lighting

Stage lighting is not an exact science. It is science in the service of performing art. Rules are few, if indeed there are any. Provided that the lighting works with the other elements in the production to enable author and actors to communicate with their audience, virtually anything goes. But even when that going is done by a particularly extreme anything, the resultant lighting will usually be a specific combination of certain possible roles that lighting can play in a production.

What can lighting contribute to a production? What are our aims when we employ light on the stage?

Illumination

Communication between actor and audience depends on sound and sight. Actors' complete bodies, but especially eyes and mouth, are their means of communication and must be clearly visible if a character is to be projected. Everything in theatre interacts and light is closely related to sound: actors who are difficult to see will usually be difficult to hear.

So the first basic requirement of stage lighting is sufficient illumination to achieve positive visibility. But how bright is that? Light is a measurable quantity but photometric measurements have little place on the stage: one of the indications of the approach of theatrical doomsday will be the appearance of a lighting designer with a photometer. Theatre is much too much of an interplay of mind and matter to be reduced to precise physical measurements. One must have confidence in the judgements of one's senses: if it looks right then it *is* right.

Unless the auditorium is very small, perhaps up to about eight rows, the amount of light cannot be ideal for all seats. If there is enough light for the front row, there will insufficient for the back: and if the amount is correct for the back row, it will be over-bright at the front. This assumes that all members of the audience have identical eyesight: which they certainly do not!

The amount of light required will vary with the brightness that has gone before. The human eye contains a mechanism, the *iris*, to adjust eye sensitivity to varying light conditions. This iris mechanism is not immediate in response and so the amount of light needed when the curtain goes up will vary with the brightness of the auditorium lights that have just gone out: the stronger the houselighting, then the stronger must be the opening stage lighting. An overture played with the houselights low or out and some light to dress the curtain – or dress the stage if there be no curtain – gives an opportunity not only to prepare audience sound sensitivity but to adjust their light responses to the scale of the production's audio-visual palette. Once the performance gets underway, the required quantity of light remains related to what has gone before. A change from relative brightness to relative darkness must take into account the time-scale of the change. A dark night scene which the audience have been watching for several minutes might be quite visible, but plunge them into such a night from a bright sunny scene and they will require a positive measure of time to readjust – and in that time, communication may be lost and the magic theatrical spell broken.

Within each stage picture, the amount of light is also relative. If one actor is brighter than another, it must be for a dramatic purpose. The seven foot tenor in the chorus who always gets his head in the light becomes the unfortunate brightness reference point for the whole stage. The usual solution is not an increase of the overall stage intensity to match the bright point, but a reduction of this over-bright part to balance with the rest of the stage. In a two-actor scene, it is often better to balance by reducing A rather than by increasing B. *Balance is the key to the amount of light required: brightness is relative rather than absolute.* If the balance is good, plotting the lighting from a mid-point in the auditorium will ensure an acceptable level for both front and back rows; but the wise lighting designer will use dress rehearsals to try seats in all parts of the house.

Light quantity is only the very beginning of the stage lighting story. After (but only after) basic illumination has been provided, light can start to fulfil a more exciting role as a dramatic tool.

Sculpture

In a conventional proscenium theatre where the audience sit in a block facing a picture-frame stage, there is a tendency for the stage picture to appear rather flat with only two dominant dimensions (width and height). The third dimension (depth) is, of course, present but less obvious. This tendency towards apparent flatness increases as the size of the auditorium increases and a larger proportion of the audience are seated further away from the stage. Indeed this is a major reason for enthusiasm for alternative theatre forms where the stage thrusts into the audience or even, as in theatre-in-the-round, becomes surrounded by the audience.

Director, designer and actor use many techniques to stress the third dimension and restore apparent depth to the production. The spacing of scenic pieces relative to one another and the use of exaggerated perspective are fundamental design techniques. Directors, often using several levels, group the actors to emphasise stage depth. But lighting designers can kill all such effort with one tiny wave of their magic wand. By pumping light flat on to the stage from the front – particularly from a low, near horizontal, angle – the stage picture can be given an appearance of total flatness.

Under flat lighting, actors' noses will not stick out and their eyes will not recede; dancers' limbs will pirouette in squashed ovals rather than true circles. But, with sympathetically angled light, actors can be presented as natural three-dimensional humans rather than as the paste-board cut-out figures which can be the inevitable product of proscenium staging.

So we must strive for a sculpturally lit actor.

With flat lighting there is little point in designing sculptural scenery. Scenic wings receiving equal frontal light will appear to run together, solid chunks will appear flat, and lumps of physical texturing will just not be visible. Solidity only becomes apparent when contrasts of light and stage are created by directional lighting.

So we must strive for a sculpturally lit scene.

But a sculpturally modelled actor in a sculpturally modelled environment is not the end of the dimensional story. There can still be a tendency for such an actor to merge with the background. By use of light, partly from the sides but especially from the back, it is possible to enhance the illusion of depth in this relationship of actor to background. It is a technique much used in the television studio where lighting makes a major contribution to restoring picture depth within the two dimensional screen. The use of backlight streaming over actors' shoulders may be difficult to justify on smaller stages where there is usually already a shortage of equipment for the more basic requirements. Nevertheless, one chunky back lighting instrument can make all the difference to the illusion of stage depth.

So we must strive for a dimensional relationship between actor and scene.

Selectivity

Film and television directors use cameras to select the exact part of the action that they wish the audience to concentrate upon at any given moment, selecting any breadth of vision from a wide panorama to a close-up of a pore on an individual's skin. In theatre, the audience normally have the whole stage within their angle of vision all the time. To focus attention on a particular area, the director can use light. The obvious technique is to light only the selected area of the stage while the rest is blacked-out. However it is also possible to make a subtle but positive selection of vision by balancing the selected area to a brighter level than the rest of the stage. It is surprising how even the smallest light re-balance can help to concentrate audience attention on the appropriate action area.

Atmosphere

Perhaps the most fascinating and rewarding use of light is the possibility of influencing the mental state of the audience. The word *atmosphere* can cover a wide range of situations. It can mean something as basic as using light to tell the audience whether the action is taking place on an October afternoon or July morning. But it can also mean something more subtle than mere weather forecasting: light can help to control whether the audience feel happy or sad, extrovert or withdrawn, aggressive or submissive.

One of the principal ways of controlling such atmosphere is by mixing warm and cool light. Warm, gold, happy and cosy at one end of the scale; cool, steel, sad and miserable at the other – but with a whole range of intermediate tones offering a continuous range of emotional response. Other possibilities include the balancing of light and shade: exaggerated contrasts can induce feelings of claustrophobia, apprehension, even terror.

But light can only *help* to create atmosphere. Light never works by itself and is only one of a package of intergrated staging devices which the production team use to control the emotional state of an audience.

Interaction

These stage lighting aims – illumination, sculpture, area selection and atmosphere creation – are not unrelated. They interact with one another to the point of positive conflict.

Atmosphere is often achieved by a partial lack of illumination. Selection of a tightly controlled area is simplest with a single spotlight: yet sculptural lighting requires a series of angles from several spotlights whose beams, ending up on the floor, will increase the size of the area selected. Lighting to enhance the third dimension can also lead to some loss of visibility unless the balance is very delicately controlled. And so on.

Adjusting light in terms of one aim usually affects the others and so lighting designers have little think-loops whizzing around in their heads while they plan and execute their lighting designs.

illumination

atmosphere   dimension

selectivity

Can I see? – do I see a sculptured actor in a sculptured environment? – do I see the correct part of the stage action? – do I sense the appropriate atmosphere? – can I *still* see? – is it *still* sculptural? – and so on.

At first one does this consciously, almost asking oneself verbal questions. But after a little experience the loop starts to accelerate and very soon it whizzes round at something approaching computer speed with a continuous assessment of all the interacting variables.

Fluidity

Stage lighting is not static. Throughout the time span of a performance, the selectivity and atmosphere of the light is fluid, with changes of two basic types: conscious and subconscious.

Typical conscious selective changes include an actor switching on a light or a rapid cross-fade from one side of the stage to the other. A typical conscious atmosphere change is a quick fade to blue for a sentimental song. The audience knows that such changes have happened and indeed may even mentally verbalise on the lines of 'Ah, the lights are changing, the sun must be setting'.

Subconscious changes are ones which the audience are not aware of, but which nevertheless influence their involvement in the production. An example of a subconscious selectivity change is the subtle shift in balance as the intensity is crept up a couple of points on one particular area and down a little on the rest of the stage: the audience attention will be concentrated on the brighter area without realising that anything has happened. Similarly, although the audience may not be aware of a smoothly slow increase of cool tone and decrease of warm, such an atmospheric shift will contribute subconsciously to the emotional effect that author, director and actor are seeking.

Cynics have been known to mutter about the stupidity of having a hundred invisible cues. But these very cues are part of the greatest excitement of true theatre: the integration of acting and related staging devices to communicate at a sub-conscious level.

Pause for a moment to consider our role as audience. It is the one moment in our lives when we sit down, lay bare our souls, and authorise someone to tamper with our subconscious and to programme our thinking. We even pay for the privilege! In our offices, factories and shops, our daily work patterns and emotional responses could be controlled by similar methods including light. If this were done we would be complaining – to put it mildly!

In a theatre, the difficulty with light changes is that individual audience members differ in their sensitivity: not just in their response to the physical optics of light, but in their general sensitivity – artistic, aesthetic, emotional, call it what you will. Thus a subconscious light movement must be very finely judged. It can never be just right for an entire audience: to some it will register consciously and to others it will penetrate not at all. This fine balance is a problem not merely for lighting: it is a basic problem of all theatrical communication.

Style

There is a danger that these lighting aims could become a rigid definition of stage lighting. But theatre is not a rigid medium: there are almost as many different possible production styles as there are productions.

In a naturalistic production aiming for accurately detailed realism, the lighting is likely to try to maintain a logic in terms of sun, moon, and table lamps. If it is a romantic play, there may be much juggling with sunset, moonrise and the switching of deli-cately shaded lamps in an attempt to create a selective atmos-phere which is logical in terms of these light sources. If the play is a farce with a complex plot of mislaid trousers, high illumination for total visibility is likely to be the prime consideration, with the only difference between midnight and high noon being that the window curtains will be closed and the room ablaze with wall brackets, table and standard lamps – or perhaps just one huge, probably imaginary, centre chandelier.

A play performed on black rostra against a cyclorama will probably treat selectivity as top priority at the relative expense of other aims. If the production is conceived in terms of gauzes, smoke and electronic music, then it is likely that the lighting style will emphasise atmosphere.

In an opera where there are lots of notes to the bar, singer's faces will go through motions not unlike those of speech and a reasonably naturalistic quality of illumination will help them to project. However, when there are lots of bars to the note a more effective approach may be to use a very atmospheric light which does not illuminate the faces too clearly: the facial contortions required to produce sustained vocal tone are not always helpful in projecting character.

Similarly in most dance situations, it is necessary to concentrate on sculptural lighting of the body as this is the dancer's principal means of dramatic expression.

One school of contemporary theatre thinking believes that the audience must be consciously, even painfully, involved in the drama: to such believers, anything savouring of a subconscious romantic atmosphere is out. Lighting becomes a continuous all-revealing blaze of white clarity. This like all other styles, is just another possible way of approaching the conversion of a script into communicative staging. The tragedy for the theatre is when any single style becomes obligatory to the point of being a matter of doctrine.

Thus, different productions will use different mixes of the standard lighting aims, and the mix for any particular production will arise from the style of that production.

A definition of stage lighting

The ideas discussed in this chapter have evolved into a possible definition of stage lighting and the words form a useful checklist of aims:

Stage lighting is a fluid selective atmospheric sculptural illumination appropriate to the style of a particular production.

2
Lighting instruments

The art may be to conceive how the production should use light in terms of the aims that we have established. The craft must be to turn such a concept into terms of lighting hardware: a palette of individual lights focused and coloured in such a way that they will combine in a series of permutations to give all the required lighting pictures. What control do we have over the light on any part of the stage?

We can control the *intensity*. The lighting control system is often referred to as the 'board', short for 'switchboard' or more correctly 'dimmerboard', since it allows us not just to select which lights are on, but to control the brightness of each one over a continuous range from maximum down to blackout.

We can control the *colour*. On the front of every stage lighting instrument there are runners to take a framed filter chosen from a vast selection of available colours.

We can control the *direction*. By choice of an appropriate physical mounting position in the theatre, we can determine the angle at which the light beam will hit the actor and/or scene.

We can control the *beam* size, shape and quality. Different types of lighting instrument allow varying adjustments of the light beam. We must choose the correct type of instrument to give the appropriate beam control required at any particular point on the stage.

We can control the *flow*. By means of the board, we can select which of the directional coloured beams are required to paint the light picture at any given moment; and by varying this selection during the time span of the production, we can produce the fluid lighting of our aims.

Thus the craft of stage lighting is the conversion of the requirements of fluid selective atmospheric sculptural illumination into the controllable elements of intensity, colour, direction, beam and flow.

INSTRUMENTS

The source of stage light is a lamp with some sort of optical system contained in a housing which incorporates a controlled means of angling. The international word for such a piece of hardware is *luminaire*. A stage luminaire is often called a *lantern* and indeed a lantern has been defined, semi-officially, as a luminaire designed or adopted for stage use. I prefer the term which originated in North America: *instrument*.

All instruments have several features in common. They all have runners to accept a colour frame and they all have a means of adjusting and fixing the vertical angle (tilt) and horizontal angle (pan). But they differ in the control that various types give over beam size, shape and quality.

FLOODS

The simplest instrument is the flood: a lamp and reflector in a box which can be panned from side to side, and tilted up and down, to control the direction of the light. There are no other adjustments: there is no means of focusing the light to control the size of the beam and there is no shuttering device to control the shape of the beam. The spread of the light, and therefore the area covered, is dependent upon the distance between the flood and the object being lit. The flood is not, therefore, a very selective instrument. Because of the lack of beam control, it is difficult to stop floods above the stage from lighting the masking borders to a greater brightness than the acting area; and floods from the side will have the same effect on scenic wings. The result is that the frame will be brighter than the picture and the eye will be pulled away from the actors.

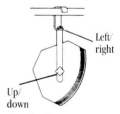

Flood adjustments

Older floods used a round screw-in tungsten lamp, backed by a simple spherical reflector. Although no longer manufactured, so many were made that they will be found on most stages for many years yet. In Britain these floods came in three principal sizes: 200, 500 and 1000 watts. These are maximum wattages, it being possible to use smaller power lamps where these are available with the appropriate size of the cap for different size lampholders. This can be an advantage on smaller stages where there is a shortage of electrical power and/or dimmer capacity. Furthermore, floods are not always chosen for size alone; each size of flood has a different reflector and will therefore give a different beam spread. For example, the old standard 1000 watt flood covered a larger area than a 500 watt flood throwing from the same distance.

Traditional flood
(*Strand Pattern 60*)

Linear flood (*CCT Minuette*)

Linear Floods

A long lamp improves horizontal light spread, and a thin lamp allows the reflector to be designed for increased vertical light spread. Therefore linear tungsten halogen lamps make possible a flood which can be used close to backcloths yet give considerable spread. The standard units for large stages are 1 kW but smaller versions using lamps of 500 watt provide a solution to many of the backcloth lighting problems common on smaller stages.

Compartment Floods

Floods can be combined during design and manufacture into multiple units with the wiring in two, three or four circuits to give a mixing possibility of two, three or four colours. When these units hang above the stage, they are known as *battens* (*borderlights* or *striplights* in some parts of the world); when sitting on the front edge of the stage they are *footlights* (or *floats* in jargon); and when placed on any other part of the stage

Traditional Batten (above)

Linear Battens (below) may be formed by linking floods together (*Teatro Diluvio S 1 kW*)

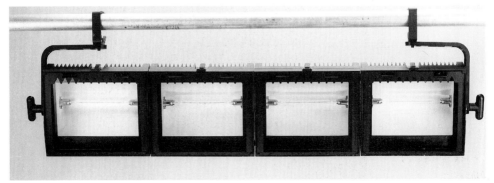

floor, the term is *electrics groundrow* – the addition of the word electrics being necessary to avoid confusion with scenic groundrow.

Floods Summarised

To summarise, flooding equipment is so unselective that its usefulness lies in the lighting of large areas of scenery such as cloths, skies, borders, and backings rather than in lighting acting areas.

SPOTS

To control the size and shape of the light beam, we need a spot-light. Spots have the same facility for pan and tilt as the flood but, additionally, there is the possibility of precise control of the angle of the emerging conical light beam and consequently of the area covered. It is convenient to group spotlights into families according to the type of beam control offered.

Focus Spots

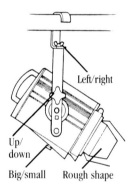

Left/right

Up/down

Big/small   Rough shape

Adjustments on focus and fresnel spots

Simple focus spots, where the lamp moves in relation to a simple plano-convex lens, were dropped from the catalogues of most Anglo-American manufacturers towards the end of the 1950s. Their light had a hardish uncontrollable edge and could be uneven unless the reflector and lamp were centred with considerable precision – and because these spots were designed before the development of prefocus lamps, this centering had to be repeated after every lamp change. The lenses used in these focus spots tended to produce a filament image in the middle of the beam and rainbows around its edge and, unless expensively heat resistant, had a habit of cracking.

However, focus spots made a reappearance at the beginning of the 1980s, using a prism-convex lens whose structure and lightly 'pebbled' surface introduces a slight diffusion which smooths the beam and gives it an edge which is positive without being either particularly hard or soft. These reincarnated focus spots have considerable application where their edge quality is appropriate and simple control of the beam size will suffice.

The beam is a cone of light, so the size of area lit increases as the *throw* distance from the spotlight to that area increases. However, the beam angle of this light cone can be altered by a focus knob which adjusts the distance between lamp and lens. As the lamp (with its reflector) is moved towards the lens, the

A simple **focus spot** with prism-convex lens (*Strand Prelude*)

beam becomes wider and as it moves away from the lens, the beam becomes narrower. On the smaller spots, this adjustment may be a simple sliding action controlled by pushing a knob backwards and forwards underneath the instrument. On larger models, there is normally a more sophisticated lead-screw device controlled by twisting a knob at the back and/or front. A *barndoor* can be slipped into the runners on the instrument: this has four rotatable shutters which offer some possibility of shaping the beam.

Focus spots are available in three sizes corresponding to lamp powers which were traditionally 500 watt, 1 kW and 2 kW. These have been augmented in recent years by 650 watt, 1.2 kW and 2.5 kW versions which seem likely to become standard. Each model has a quoted spread of beam angles, with about 4°–8° as minimum and 60° as maximum.

Focus spots summarised

To summarise, the simple focus spot with a PC lens gives control of the size of the beam and a barndoor gives some control of the beam shape. But there is no adjustment for beam quality: by selecting a simple focus spot, we are opting for a softish yet positively defined edge.

Fresnel Spots

The fresnel lens has a characteristic 'stepped' moulding on one face and is textured on the reverse. This produces a very even light which is soft at the edges and tends to project a soft shadow. Because the edge of the light is soft, it is not absolutely precise and therefore blends easily with the edges of similar spots to give a smooth coverage.

Fresnel with barndoor (*CCT Minuette*)

In addition to giving this soft edge to the beam, a fresnel lens has a tendency to cast some low-intensity light outside the main

beam: such spill light can be a nuisance if the instrument is close to a scenery border or wing. The spill of scatter light can be controlled by a *barndoor* which may also be used to give some shape to the beam by introducing up to four straight soft edges.

For many years the standard British fresnels were 500 watt with 6 inch lens and a 1 kW with 8 inch lens. For very short throws there was a 4½ inch lens using a 250 or 500 watt lamp, and for high budget long throws a 10 inch with an option of 1 kW or 2 kW lamp. As so many of these were made during the period when stage lighting was expanding and new stages being built, they are likely to remain in use for many years yet. Some of these fresnel spots were supplied with lenses where a black coating had been baked on to the vertical steps of the lens to reduce scatter. However the small reduction in scatter light from these *colouvred* lenses was found to be not worth the resultant loss of light in the main beam – or indeed the extra cost of the colouvred lens.

The newer fresnel spots are more compact and use smaller diameter lenses. These tend to have rather more scatter than the earlier models and so a barndoor becomes essential. It is important to plan sufficient space for the length of the instrument plus barndoor when hanging over the stage since the corners of the barndoors have a nasty habit of catching on cloths and gauzes: this often results in a tear, as well as knocking the light off its setting. Like focus spots, fresnels are now becoming standardised on tungsten halogen lamps of 650 watt, 1.2 kW and 2.5 kW. The manufacturer's catalogues include details of the maximum and minimum spread through which each model can be adjusted, with 7° to around 50°–60° being typical.

Fresnels summarised

To summarise, the fresnel spot offers control of the size of the beam and a barndoor can add some control of the beam shape. But fresnels have no adjustment for beam quality: by selecting a fresnel, we are opting for a soft beam with a very soft undefined edge.

Profile Spots

In a profile spot, the lamp and reflector remain stationary while the lens is movable (whereas in a focus or fresnel spot, the lens is stationary and it is the lamp and reflector which move). The lens movement in a profile spot controls the *beam quality*: the lenses produce a very hard precise edge which can be gradually

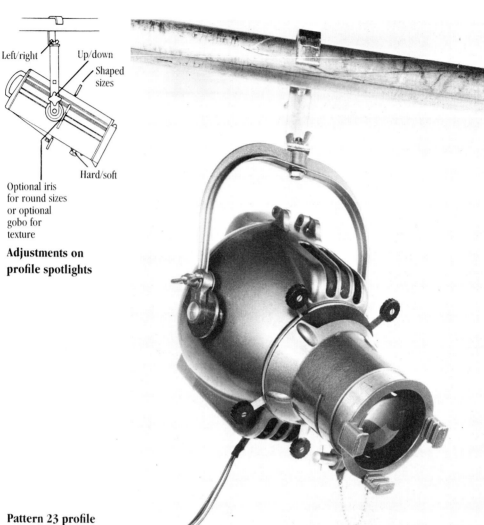

Left/right

Up/down

Shaped sizes

Hard/soft

Optional iris
for round sizes
or optional
gobo for
texture

**Adjustments on
profile spotlights**

**Pattern 23 profile
spot**

softened by progressive movement of the lens tube. Control of
beam *size* and *shape* in standard profile spots is by adjustments
at the central point of the optical system known as the *gate*. At
this point, all profile spots have a series of four shutters which
can be used to make any size of four-sided shape. There is a slot
with runners which accept either an iris diaphragm to give a full
range of circular beam sizes, or a metal mask to produce any required beam size and shape.

The profile spot is so-called because it will project a profile
of whatever two-dimensional shape is placed in the gate
runners; and that profile can be projected to any required

degree of hardness/softness by movement of the lens. A mask for use in the gate is known as a *gobo* and because of the intense heat at this point in the instrument, gobos must be made from heat resistant material. Do-it-yourself gobos can be made from the pliable alloys used for baking pies in domestic ovens.

Commercial gobo manufacturers use a photolithography process which enables any two-dimensional image to be reproduced as a cutout in heat-resistant alloy. Gobos may be selected from comprehensive catalogues or custom made from design drawings. Standard gobo ranges include such specific images as windows, trees and the Eiffel Tower. However a major gobo application is break-up patterns which, with softish focusing, introduce a texture into the light beam.

Moving the lens to adjust edge quality also produces some variations in beam size. Getting the best performance from a profile spot usually requires simultaneous adjustment of lens and shutters but, unless the electrician is an octopus, this has to be done by fiddling with shutters and lens alternately.

Most profile spots also have a screw arrangement to make

A profile spot (left) will project the line pattern of a **gobo**, placed in the optical 'gate' between the lamphouse and lenses.

Gobos (**below**) may be definite images or simple break up patterns which will give the effect of dappled light or, according to the softness of focus, a feeling of texture.

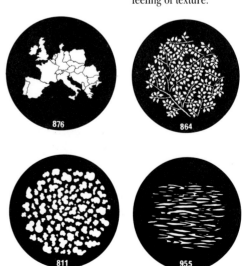

fine adjustments of the lamp in relation to the optical system. This allows the beam to be finely tuned between an even intensity or a hot centre.

To allow for easier adjustment of edges, some older profile spots have two sets of shutters. In addition to the normal shutters at the optical centre, these spots (sometimes called bifocal) have another set of shutters which have serrated edges and are positioned just behind the optical gate. When the lens is focused to produce hard edges from the normal shutters, the extra shutters produce soft edges. Such a double shutter arrangement makes for easier selection of edge quality and allows for a mixture of hard and soft edges in the same beam.

The shuttering and masking devices in profile spots convert a lot of unused energy into heat. It is sensible, therefore, to use the correct lenses to produce the required beam size with the minimum use of shutters. Ideally shutters should be used to trim the beam edge rather than to cut it down to size and this means selecting the appropriate lens for the throw distance between instrument and stage.

The Leko, long synonymous with profile spotlighting in North America has become an international standard in its current diecast form. A wide range of lens options allows selection of an instrument with the optimum beam angle for any particular job. (*Lekos*, now marketed worldwide by Strand Lighting were developed by Century Lighting Inc., although the term became something of a generic name for profile spots with an ellipsoidal reflector.)

Variable Beam Profile Spots

The limited beam variation of a simple profile spot reduces the flexibility of any rig, particularly a permanent rig which has to be capable of rapid refocusing to the requirements of different productions. *Variable beam profile spots* use a type of zoom arrangement where differential movement of two lenses allows control of wide variations in both beam size and quality. The shutters are then only required for beam shaping.

Standardisation on small compact tungsten halogen lamps as a light source has enabled a degree of modular construction. One manufacturer has developed a system whereby standard lamphouses can be coupled to alternative lens tubes. Other manufacturers use standardised die castings and extrusions to house several fixed and variable beam options in a range of instruments based on a common approach to optical and mechanical design.

Optical systems for profile spots are designed to use either radially or axially mounted lamps. The essential difference is that radials sit base down in front of the rear reflector, while axials are mounted through a hole in the centre of the reflector. Axial mounting generally produces more light, although there can be lamp life problems at higher voltages. Consequently, axial mounting finds rather more favour in countries operating at 110 volts than those with 240 volts.

Variable angle models have become the standard profile spots for new installations. They use the same range of halogen lamp wattages as the other families of spotlights discussed above. At each wattage there are models offering different

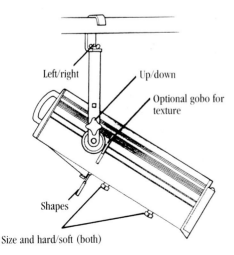

Left/right

Up/down

Optional gobo for texture

Shapes

Size and hard/soft (both)

Adjustments on variable beam profile spots

options of variable beam angle range, such as 16°–30° or 28°–40°. However, many theatres continue to use some of the older simple profiles with which they were originally equipped, particularly 1 kW bifocals which were the standard auditorium

In the **Strand Cantata** series of variable beam profile spotlights a pair of independently adjustable lenses offer a wide variation in beam angle and edge quality from a single instrument. Cantatas use a 1.2 kW lamp and have a rotating gate to simplify shutter angling.

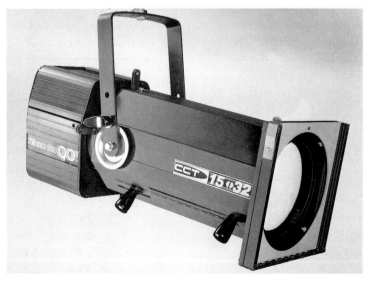

The **CCT Silhouette 90** range of variable beam profile spotlights allows alternative lens tubes (11–26° or 15–32° or 19–45°) to be fitted to alternative (1/1.2 kW or 2 kW or 2.5 kW) lamphouses

spot throughout the decade of expansion from the mid 1960s to the mid 1970s. Also, despite all the recent advances in mechanical and optical design, the 500 watt Pattern 23 (introduced in the early 1950s and manufactured for 30 years) remains a robust compact instrument with the promise of quite a considerable life hereafter.

Profiles summarised

To summarise, the profile spot controls the size and shape of the beam by adjustment of built-in shutters or insertion of a gobo. Movement of the lens controls the beam quality by softening the hard edge as required. In the variable angle versions, differential movement of the two lenses controls both beam size and quality. Profile spots scatter much less light outside the main beam than fresnels or focus spots.

DIFFUSERS

Diffuser filters placed in front of an instrument's lens smooth the light beam and soften its edge. It is likely that the recent development of increasingly subtle diffusers, such as Rosco 164 and 119, will have a considerable influence on the way we use spotlights. By choice of appropriate strengths of diffusion, a PC focus spot can be softened progressively until the light quality is equivalent to a fresnel. Consequently the PC can be regarded as a much more flexible instrument than the fresnel.

The use of diffusers in profile spots, particularly 119 for short throws and 164 for long throws, allows the lenses to be set for hard edges which is certainly faster and also tends to make more efficient use of the optics.

BEAMLIGHTS

The most difficult light quality to control is the visibility of the actual beam passing through the air. So far, all our references to beam control have been in terms of what happens when the light hits an actor or scenery. Sometimes we wish to see a light beam stabbing through the air and making the direction of source obvious; more often we would prefer just to see the stage lit without much indication of the multiple sources that are providing the light. Either way it should be a *controlled* situation. Unfortunately, in most cases, whether we see the

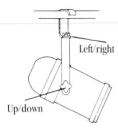

Adjustments on beamlights. A focus knob allows the lamp to be centred in the reflector for smoothest beam; parcan lamps may be rotated for orientation of the non-circular beam.

Left/right

Up/down

500w low voltage beamlight (*Strand*)

beam or not depends on air pollution rather than the instrument. To be seen, the light must reflect off something and so beam visibility will depend on the quality of dust and moisture in the air. The increased prohibition of audience smoking and the advent of air conditioning have contributed to making beams invisible. No longer do we have the spectacle of a stage criss-crossed with stabbing searchlights on foggy evenings in city theatres where smoking was permitted.

The one instrument type where the beam shows up better than others is the *beamlight*. Whereas PC, fresnel and profile spots have conical beams lighting an area whose size increases in proportion to throw distance, the beamlight has a parallel beam so that the size of area lit remains fixed whatever the throw. This parallel beam is produced by using a parabolic reflector and no lens; it responds well to any particles suspended in the air and will always be more dramatically visible than other types of instrument beam. Central Europe has a tradition of beamlights (mostly 500 watt, but also 1 kW) with 24 volt lamps fed from a transformer built into the instrument casing. In Britain 1 kW beamlights at 240 volt have long been common, but until recently low voltage versions had to be imported.

Parcans

Perhaps one of the most interesting light sources developments of recent years is the PAR lamp with reflector and lens sealed within the same glass envelope as the filament. The Parcan is a simple can to hold this 'sealed beam lamp' and provide facilities for suspension, pan, tilt and colour filter. There is no provision for focusing since beam size, shape and quality are determined by choice of lamp. The beams of these lamps are oval with a choice of a tight nearly parallel spot or varying degrees of a wider more flooded beam. The narrower the beam, the more intense the light. The lamps can be rotated within the can to make optimum use of the oval beam shape. The brightest 1 kW Par lamps operate at 120 volts and so they are frequently used as series-connected pairs on 240 volt supplies. The intense light makes them very suitable for backlight when they create a depth enhancing haze in the space surrounding the actor. Their intensity also ensures that considerable brightness can still be achieved with the deepest saturated colour filters.

Parcan (*Thomas*)

Light Curtains

A row of very tight intense par beams, vertical or slightly back-lighting, produces something approaching a solid wall of light. Most light curtains use low voltage par lamps wired in series to enable them to be operated from a standard mains voltage dimmer. The success of a light curtain's haze in obscuring whatever is behind it depends particularly on good control of floor reflections and on the presence of smoke and moisture particles in the air.

SMOKE

In situations where its presence is stylistically appropriate – or at least acceptable – smoke is sometimes introduced to help make light beams visible. Smoke generators are discussed in Chapter 17.

FOLLOW SPOTS

Most follow spots (often referred to as 'limes'), which an operator uses to follow the actor around the stage, are basically profile spots with a rather more sophisticated optical and mechanical design. They have to be particularly well balanced to allow smooth pan and tilt; and controls for iris and focus must lie naturally under the operator's hand. To achieve high intensity, follow spots often use discharge lamps and they are focused with a very hard edge because the follow spot, particularly in Anglo-American lighting, has become a mark of star-status rather than a mere source of light.

Beamlights have long been used in central European opera houses for discreet following – delicately boosting selective visibility rather than consciously drawing attention to star actors. The parallel beam giving automatic head to waist coverage independent of throw distance, plus the soft quality of the beam edge, allow the operator to concentrate totally on following without having to make adjustments of iris and lenses. This type of following is becoming common in musicals.

LAMPS

Three types of light source are in normal use: tungsten, tungsten-halogen and discharge. In passing, it should be noted that fluorescent lamps have very little application on the stage: although very efficient in terms of energy usage, a long tubular source of diffused light is difficult to incorporate optically or mechanically in an instrument designed for projection of a controlled beam. However stage lighting is a broad church from which no source should be excluded: some of the more experimental lighting styles using a small number of highpowered

Teatro Talento Follow spot with 1200 MSR discharge lamp has integral iris, colour magazine and interchangeable lenses for a variety of beam angles. Balance is adjustable.

non-conventional instruments have included fluorescent tubes to dramatic effect.

Discharge lamps (such as CSI, CID or HMI) cannot be dimmed by normal electrical means and are therefore mostly confined to such applications as manually-operated follow spots and scenic projectors. It is possible to dim instruments using discharge lamps by fitting remotely controlled motorised shutters. While this may seem cumbersome and expensive, it becomes viable when other functions of the instrument – pan, tilt, focus and colour change – are being subjected to remote motor control.

The tungsten lamps used in stage lighting are big brothers of the familiar domestic lamps. Being more highly powered, they are designed to overcome problems arising from the extra heat generated. To ensure that the filament lines up precisely with the instrument's optics, modern spotlight lamps have a special

Arri spotlight with discharge lamp (1.2 kW HMI) **and mechanical dimmer.**

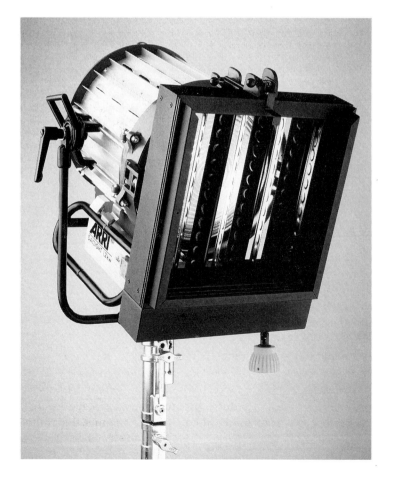

pre-focus cap: the domestic bayonet cap (BC) is virtually un-known and the screw cap (ES or GES) is confined to situations with uncritical optics such as floods and compartment battens.

The light output of tungsten lamps gradually decreases throughout their life while tungsten halogen lamps maintain their original light output throughout life. Another advantage of halogen lamps is that they are physically small and this simplifies optical and mechanical design of lighting instruments. Also, standardisation on a small range of compact halogen lamps simplifies stock-holding. Every possible permutation of long, short, thin, fat, cap-up, cap-down was known in the tungsten series and so a special lamp had to be stocked for each type of instrument.

Every lamp design has to compromise between light output and life: if one goes down, the other goes up. Nevertheless, as a general rule most lamps find a compromise that ensures a

brighter light for a longer life than the corresponding tungsten lamps – with the bonus that the brighter light is maintained throughout life. The user, however, can often opt for a lamp that will increase either life or light at the expense of the other. Halogen lamps with special bases have therefore become standard for all new instruments. Ordinary tungsten lamps are still available for most older spotlights although the user has an option to fit special halogen lamps with prefocus bases and a glass envelope structure which lines the filament up with the instruments optics. For older equipment on small stages there is still something in favour of ordinary tungsten lamps: their initial cost is less and there is not a lot of virtue in extending life if the equipment only has occasional use. Furthermore, there is little

Small compact halogen lamps allow a full range of optics to be packaged in a uniform style. The **Strand Quartet** range includes (from left to right) a fresnel, a prism convex, a profile [25°] and a variable beam profile [22–45°].

point in maintaining brightness throughout life if little-used lenses and reflectors gradually acquire a coating of dust: there are many situations where spotlights only get cleaned when their lamps are changed.

NEW TECHNOLOGY

The development of stage lighting has been particularly rapid since the end of the 1950s. Advances in lighting instruments have perhaps not been quite so spectacular as those in control boards, but there have been continuous advances in the sophistication of profile spots and in light sources.

New technologies have to be assessed against two basic criteria: their potential for improvements in

(a) design quality *and*

(b) design management.

The latter, being more capable of objective analysis, is easier to quantify with new equipment bringing savings in time and money. The financial savings involve spending capital in order to save running costs. Some improvements in design quality are also related to savings in time since part of the saved time can be allocated to scheduling experiment. Moreover new technologies tend to bring humanitarian benefits by reducing physical labour, resulting in a lighting crew whose wits are sharpened by being less tired. Lighting alchemists dream of a new cheap bright light, generating no heat, with wire-less remote control of colour, direction, intensity, beam angle and shutters – and preferably with a beam that turns corners and stops after it reaches an actor! Some of this is even possible!

Remote Control

A particularly exciting development area is remote control of pan, tilt, focus and colour. Remote colour changing by motorised wheels or solenoid operated semaphores has been common for at least fifty years – usually offering a choice of four filters or open white. And remote control of pan and tilt movements is not new. Rods, tracker wires, chains and bicycle brake cables are all mechanical devices with an honourable history almost as long as spotlights themselves. Motors with up/down/ stop pushes were soon applied, particularly by the Germans, and by 1960 the degrees of each movement could be preset by means of polarised relays. By the mid-1970s these functions could be memorised: it is particularly uncanny to watch a spot

The **Rainbow Scroller** (Camelont AB of Sweden) allows a light to be provided with a magazine of eleven colours. With a scroll time of approximately one second, selection is so fast as to be virtually instantaneous.

bar resetting itself with all the spotlights changing all their functions (pan, tilt, focus, colour) simultaneously.

Such equipment is necessarily bulky and very expensive: until recently it was to be found mainly in German opera houses on upstage lighting bars with difficult access. This remote operation is intended for refocusing instruments when they are unlit – possibly between cues, probably between scenes and certainly between productions in repertoire theatres which play different performances each night while rehearsing yet another one during the day. The justification for expenditure here is mostly lighting management – rapid resetting without access.

Systems such as Strand Lighting's PALS allow any conventional spotlight to be supplied with remote operation of pan, tilt, focus or iris and optional colour scroller. All positions for each change are recorded on a memory control desk and fed to the lights by digital signals along a single pair of wires.

The popular music industry has a purely lighting design requirement in that it is concerned with movement which will be visually effective during a scene. Rock bands in particular demand a lighting style where movement of the lamps is almost the norm, with stillness being reserved for an occasional dramatic effect. In such concerts the lighting rig, with the loudspeaker stacks, is also the scenery. Sometimes the movement is produced by motorised mirrors which deflect the beam in fast gyrations. Sometimes the colour is multi-changed by scroll colour changers where around a dozen colours can be taped together for very fast changes.

A more radical development is the *VARI*LITE* which uses

The **Strand PALS** version of their *Cadenza PC* allows remote control of pan, tilt and focus. An optional colour scroller may be fitted.

motors to pan through 360° and tilt through 270°with a rotation time from 0.75° to 240° per second. An immensely bright light is produced by a discharge lamp and since this cannot be dimmed electrically, it is faded by a motorised mechanical shutter. One model has an integral wheel for 9 interchangeable gobos and the internal dichroic colour wheels offer a virtually unlimited choice of colours from pastel tints to saturates. All functions are controlled by digital information signals transmitted along a single wire.

Discharge Lamps

The attraction of discharge lamps is that they provide a very bright light from relatively little electricity. But they cannot be dimmed by reducing the electricity to the lamp in the normal way: indeed they need a momentary jab of very high voltage to make the light 'strike' and appear. However, they can be dimmed by a mechanical shutter which is positioned appropriately in the optical system so that it fades softly (rather than with the hard edges of shutters placed at the optical centre of a profile spot). For the particularly subtle fading required in a scenic projector, glasses progressively darkened from clear to

The **VARI*LITE VL4, with a 400 watt HTI discharge lamp**, has remote pan and tilt which is variable in speed from 240° to .75° per second. The beam angle is from 4° to 28° and textured glass panels provide a range of diffusion. 240 colours are pre-programmed and any further mixture of the internal cyan, magenta and amber dichroic filters is possible. Colour crossfades can be as instant as .3 seconds or last for hours.

black can be moved across the slide. Such mechanical contrivances might seem tiresomely complicated but with today's technology there is no difficulty in running a ring main supply around several spots and controlling the dimmer shutter (and other functions) by digital information from the control desk's microprocessor. Certainly the light output makes this kind of technology an attractive proposition.

Low Voltage

Low voltage lamps give a much more intense light than mains voltage lamps of the same wattage. The drawback is the chunky weight of the conventional transformer which has to be included in the instrument. However the latest toroidal transformers are somewhat smaller and lighter, and electronic transformers promise exciting possibilities for the future.

Heat and Fans

The future of lighting instruments has one major problem to which no effective solution is in sight – heat. Lamps generate heat which has to be dissipated carefully to avoid light leaks through ventilation holes. With discharge lamps and integral electronic transformers in particular, this heat has to be dissipated with particular efficiency. Fans are permissible in follow spots and scene projectors but not normally in the rig for any production with spoken dialogue. It may be possible to make a silent prototype fan for one instrument, but we await an easily maintained fan which will still be silent when there is a batch of twenty on a spot bar.

3
Lighting control

The operation of dimming systems has become very much simplified in the past couple of decades, first by the introduction of electronics and then by the application of microprocessor based information technology. Primitive mechanical units, requiring considerable muscular effort from rather more limbs than normal humans possess, have been superseded by small electronic desks offering fingertip control. Indeed mass production techniques have brought the industry to a point where it is no longer economic to catalogue mechanical systems as they would be more expensive than an electronic package which does a better job. However, just because equipment has been dropped from the catalogue does not mean that it is no longer in use. But there is now little demand, even on the smallest stages, for the virtuoso octopus who can operate mechanical dimmer handles with simultaneous movements of hands, feet, elbows, knees, chin and even forehead!

Remote Control

The main functions of a lighting control system are, firstly, to act as a central point for the distribution of electricity to the various instruments; and, secondly, to control the stage picture by varying the amount of each light's electricity, and therefore its brightness, at any given moment. Ideally, the control should be positioned where the operator has a clear view of the stage action. This, however, is not usually an ideal position for a central electricity distribution point. In the older directly-operated boards, the control and distribution of the heavy electrical loads took place in the same unit and this normally had to be installed in an on-stage position conveniently placed for relatively short cable runs to the lights. Such a dimmerboard could be placed in a control room at the rear of the auditorium but this was seldom done because, apart from the excessive cable costs, the gymnastics required to operate the bulky machine made it difficult to even observe the stage action, let alone concentrate upon it.

Electronic systems are two-part. The actual dimming takes place in a unit which can be placed at any convenient point for distribution. These dimmers are controlled remotely from a compact desk and, as the information is carried from desk to dimmers by very small control currents, the inter-connection cable can be thin and long. Indeed, the latest digital technology allows the information to be sent along a single slender wire. So modern control equipment can be placed in the most convenient position to meet both electrical and operational requirements.

Channels, Ways and Ratings

A control *channel* consists of

(1) a control surface – the miniature lever or other device that we operate to alter the light intensity,
(2) the interconnecting control cable to the solid state dimmer,
(3) the dimmer itself,
(4) the protective fuse,
(5) the heavy load wiring running from the dimmer to a socket in a specific position in the theatre *and*
(6) that socket or sockets.

Each such channel has a specified rating in kilowatts and will control any load consisting of one or more instruments, provided that their total kilowattage does not exceed the specified kilowatt rating of the channel. A significant feature of the electronic revolution in lighting intensity control is that, whereas the old mechanical resistance dimmers could only deal smoothly with loads between rather finely stated limits, modern thyristor dimmers can handle any load from a few watts up to their rated maximum. This is normally between 2 and 2.5 kW, although some larger installations have a proportion of 5 or 6 kW dimmers. Channels are sometimes referred to as circuits, and a control system is often described as 'X-ways' where X is the number of channels. Thus a system with 20 channels is called a '20-way'.

Cues and Cue States

A light change involving intensity alterations is known as a *cue (Q)*. The various static pictures between such changes are known as *cue states*. A cue therefore represents lighting on the move whereas a cue state is lighting in repose. A cue where the channels generally increase in brightness is known as a *build* while a general reduction in brightness levels is called a *check*. Sometimes build and check are referred to as fade-up and fade-down and a cue with some channels increasing while others decrease is a *cross-fade*.

Presetting

If a control desk has only a small number of channels, perhaps up to about a dozen, a nimble-fingered operator might just about be able to cope with a cue where most of the levers do a slow check or build. However a cross-fade in five seconds might not be very smooth! To overcome this problem, all modern systems, large and small, make a feature of *presetting*. On manual preset desks, every channel has at least two levers, three is common, and there can be more. Each such set of levers is called a preset and each preset is controlled by a *master*. When a master is at zero, its preset does not influence the dimmers and any movement of the channel levers on that preset will not affect the lights. The preset levers can therefore be set (or 'pre-set' – hence the terminology) to the levels required in a cue state. The cue to achieve this cue state can then be performed smoothly by the one-handed action of moving the master from

Two preset portable desk with dipless cross-fader. (*Strand Tempus*)

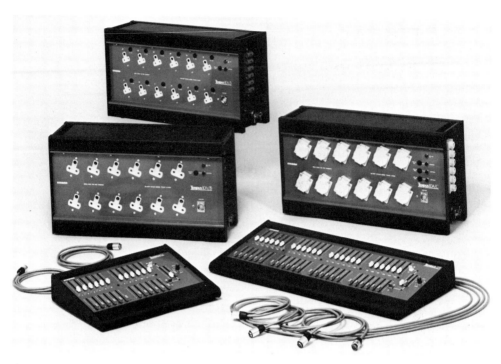

6-way dimmer packs with 12 and 24 channel desks. Each dimmer is rated to control up to 2 kW. (*Strand Tempus* system.)

zero to full, at the speed required to complete the change in the plotted time.

The next cue state can then be prepared on another preset which has its master at zero. By fading one master and building the other, the lighting picture represented by the first preset is replaced by the lighting prepared on the second. Presets obey the law of 'highest takes precedence': if more than one preset is active at the same time with masters at full, the brightness of any particular channel will be the setting of that channel's highest individual preset lever.

Grouping

To give increased facilities, particularly to allow a cue to be divided into separately timed and possibly overlapping parts, presets are often divided into groups. Each channel may be allocated to a group by means of switching. The switches may be one per channel, in which case a particular channel is on the same group in all presets. Or there may be a set of channel switches for each preset to allow channels to be grouped differently in each of the presets. Another method is to use a pin matrix allowing the formation of a larger number of groups than the two or three which are practical with simple switching.

Crossfading

In addition to preset and group masters, most desks are fitted with a *dipless crossfade*. By moving this master at the desired speed, a smooth transition from one scene to another can be accomplished without the visual dip that is difficult to eliminate when using individual preset masters to crossfade between two presets with several common channels.

MEMORIES AND COMPUTERS

The possible number of presets in a manual system is theoretically infinite but operational convenience places a limit at about four. Beyond this, it is easier and cheaper to adapt the memory storage systems of computer technology. Such systems are essentially infinite preset controls where, instead of setting up rows of channel levers, the necessary information is stored automatically under a file number and retrieved at the touch of a button. Operating a memory system is like operating the masters of a manual system without having to worry about setting up presets physically.

Early memory boards used such electro-mechanical devices as punch cards, drums, discs or tape for data storage of dimmer levels. However all current systems are based on solid state electronic memories without any moving parts. Any use of disc or tape is now confined to library storage of plots for a series of productions in repertoire theatres where they are used for programming the memories prior to a performance rather than in operating the performance. Reliability has increased steadily while prices keep falling as a result of the micro-processor revolution. Consequently, memory boards are now standard equipment for even the smallest professional stages, with only an occasional small manual preset board being found under studio conditions.

A memory system has three essential parts:
(1) channel access,
(2) record *and*
(3) playback.
There are several possible methods of 'channel access'. Perhaps the most obvious is the use of a lever for each channel. Columns of pushes for hundreds, tens and units have also been used successfully. But the most popular method, in an age when pocket calculators have become commonplace, is to use a

Two preset manual control (12, 24 or 48 channels) **with memory facilities** (*Strand MX*)

Compact micro-processor lighting control with keyboard channel access. (*Strand M24*)

keyboard in which the channel can not only be called up but given a level – e.g. tapping 2 – 7 – at – 5 will bring channel 27 – 50%. This is not 50% light but the halfway point on a scale of 1 to 10 or 100 where the points represent progress along a dimmer curve which has been selected to give a smooth control, compensating for the abrupt changes that would otherwise occur near the fully on and fully off positions. Associated with such a keyboard is a wheel type lever by which any selected channel can be eased up or down from its existing level.

When the desired cue state is reached by balancing channels in this way, it is recorded in an electronic 'file'. The digital keyboard has also become the most popular method of selecting a file number. Sometimes there is a separate keyboard for this memory 'record' but frequently one keyboard shares the options of 'channel' and 'memory' by a push button selection.

To 'playback' any memory it is routed via another set of pushes to the appropriate masters. Many memory systems have two playbacks so that two sets of cues may be run simultaneously – perhaps a slow general fade continuing on one playback while a series of faster area changes are performed on the other playback. Some playbacks have single lever crossfaders giving a smooth dipless transition from one memorised state to another. But most playbacks have paired faders with one lever for the incoming channels and another for the outgoing, so that one can lead or lag the other if required. These faders are usually mounted together so that they can be operated with one hand for a dipless crossfade. At any time during a cue, the operator can select any individual channels for independent adjustment if necessary. On some systems the cue is instigated by a push, and the faders used only to speed up or slow down the progress of the cue.

Various methods of displaying information to the operator are used. The most common is a series of numerical windows plus a VDU (Video Display Unit). One numerical window is associated with each keyboard to show the last number selected. There are usually two with each playback: one to show the file number of the memorised state now holding the light on stage, while the other displays the number of the next state selected (i.e. preset) for substitution by a movement (i.e. cue) of that playback's master. The VDU can show all sorts of data, the most important being the intensity level for each channel, with these level numbers changing as a cue progresses. There is a growing tendency to use only a video display and, while this is in line with everyday computer operation experience, I personally feel that numerical window displays are easier to read during a long lighting rehearsal.

There is virtually no limit to the facilities that can be incorporated in a computerised lighting board: multiple playbacks, automatic sequencing, library storage and print-out are all common features of the larger boards. Most systems include a

Strand Light Palette 90 – a high performance desk for the operator who prefers a lighting control to respond rather more like a computer than a traditional theatre board.

Strand Galaxy 3 provides major theatres with a particularly extensive range of facilities which can include integrated control of remotely operated spotlights.

back-up to keep the performance alive if the machine breaks down. This can take the form of a simple pin patch to bring essential groups under special masters, or a separate manual presetting desk. The more complex systems have sufficient duplication of components to ensure that (as in the hydraulics systems of an aircraft) there is never a total breakdown. The

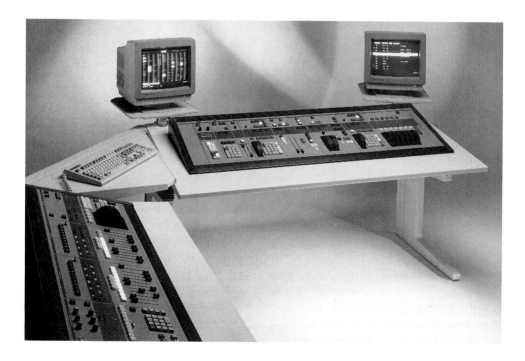

most sophisticated back-up is to have a complete second system running in tandem, ready for instant takeover if the primary system fails.

TIMING

With the older directly operated dimmers, timing was the major problem. The amount of preparation possible between cues was strictly limited and consisted mainly of memorising (in the operator's brain, not a computer!) the actions which would be required when the cue began. Once started on a ten second cue with several levers moving to different positions, there was little time to study a written plot and, with several dimmers moving simultaneously, little chance to introduce subtleties into the timing. The operator could only aim hopefully for overall smoothness, with the final half-a-point subtleties still being tweaked into place after the main cue time had elapsed. Many fascinating engineering solutions were devised to solve the operational problems, but they now belong to history.

The principal virtue of all remotely-controlled electronic dimming systems is that they allow the operator to concentrate on timing the flow of light during a performance. Both manual presetting and memory make it possible for all the routine work to be done as a preparation between cues, so that when the cue starts the operator need be concerned only with the finer nuances of timing. Although a cue may be labelled as, say, 15 seconds, this is unlikely to be a straight mathematical count. It may start slowly, then accelerate and finally even out; or perhaps the opposite way round. The important point is that the timing is probably the sum of a series of individual rates which operators, like actors, must feel in their theatrical bones, because the subtle variations in timing from one performance to another, from one audience to another, are what makes a live performance truly alive.

Some manual preset desks have an optional automatic timer so that the cue time can be preset (i.e. the length of the cue not the moment when it begins). Micro-processor desks have this automatic timing recorded in their memory. However, this is always arranged so that the operator can take over manual control instantly. Many operators prefer to ignore such automatic timing facilities except in very slow fades. The most critical point in any fade is the point where lamps coming from zero may jump after a delay while the filament heats. One manufacturer includes a 'pre-heat' facility to compensate for this and others have developed programmes to memorise the 'profile' of a cue – i.e. the way in which its rate accelerates and decelerates during its progress. But all this can be done by the operator and I would always prefer to entrust the finer details of timing to operator sensitivity. Modern lighting controls are very sophisticated instruments and their operators are performing artists.

ROCK BOARDS

While many boards are splendid for reproducing the cue states of pre-plotted lighting, and providing sophisticated facilities to enable fluid progression through these states under full operator control of the timing, they tend to lack the necessary flexibility for 'instant' lighting design. For instant lighting of un-plotted one-night-stands, the group facilities of complex systems or the back-ups of simpler ones are often sufficient.

However, the dynamic lighting requirements of rock bands and industrial presentations, where the lighting designer normally operates the show, require a different kind of flexibility. In particular there is a need to be able to balance several groups, to flash channels singly or in groups and to set up complex chase sequences. This requirement is best served by a 'lever-per-channel' access where each channel dimmer lever has an associated flash button plus facilities for selection to group masters/flashers and allocation to sequence modes. In the latest

Rock boards offer maximum flexibility for fluid lighting of performances where sequential playback of pre-plotted cues is inappropriate. (*Avolites QM 500* console for 180 channels, with 400 memories available on 20 faders, together with simple programming for complex chase patterns.)

rock boards, each fader lever can, as an alternative to controlling a single channel, have a memorised picture assigned to it. Such a desk is laid out so that the operator, with help from a few labels, is able to remember which knobs work which lights — and so play the lighting board as if it were a musical instrument.

NEW CONTROL TECHNOLOGIES

Desks for intensity control have probably developed just about as far as they need to go. Indeed it could be said that some of them have developed further than necessary. Each new system on the market is received as a new challenge. On every lighting manufacturers stand at every technical theatre exhibition, operators can be found pitting their wits against the latest control to discover what it will not do. As microprocessors can be programmed to tell dimmers to do virtually anything, the facilities on boards just grow and grow. Many of these facilities are very rarely required but it is fine to have them available provided they do not get in the way of simple operation of essential basics. My own priorities for intensity control development are therefore not more complex facilities but

(a) ergonomics,

(b) reliability *and*

(c) price.

Arri Impuls combines facilities for both instant light mixing and complex plotting. Each of the 108 faders may control single channels or act as submasters, each with two memorised lighting states.

Control Surfaces

The traditional interface between the operator's finger and the control desk's functions are lever, wheel and push button. Some systems have tried the computer's light pen and mouse, but with little operator enthusiasm. Joysticks have met with little success as master crossfade levers (sideways movement being used to profile the fade progress) but they may have some potential for instrument movements. Various experiments are

The **Arri Designer's Graphic Tablet** allows instant access to any channel or group by using a stylus to touch the appropriate symbol on a drawing which may utilise any form of graphic representation favoured by the lighting designer – such as plans, plots, sketches, etc.

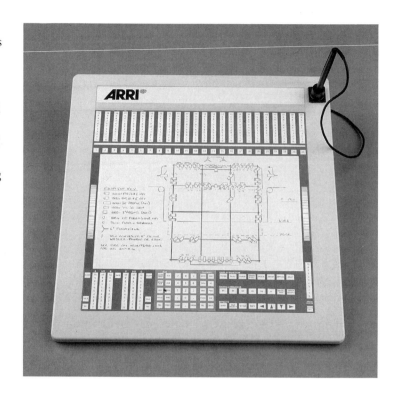

taking place – always with better 'playability' as the goal. Many involve touch sensitive surfaces, usually laid out geographically, sometimes in terms of the position of the light but often, and perhaps more fundamentally, in terms of where the light falls.

Additional Control Functions

The major area for control system development is in functions other than intensity. In the previous chapter we have noted how remotely controlled pan, tilt, focus and colour filter scrollers are being fitted to conventional halogen spotlights. Using even more radical technology are the new instruments based on discharge lamps which, being non-dimmable electrically, require remotely operated mechanical dimming shutters. The potential for such features as integral selection and rotation of gobos and virtually infinite colouring range of colouring extend lighting desk flexibility far beyond the traditional control of intensity.

It is not yet clear how the facilities in the lighting control room will develop to accommodate these new demands. It seems desirable that all control functions should be coordinated from one desk – certainly as far as performance playback is concerned. However, rather than have all activities integrated in one desk, it may be more appropriate for some of the newer functions to have their own control systems whose cue actions are triggered by the master 'go' button on the main desk. This could offer faster plotting and rehearsing possibilities, and it would permit users to assemble the system most appropriate for their needs, taking advantage of new technologies as they develop.

Digital Dimmers

Since the thyristor revolutionised dimming in the mid-1960s most dimmer development has been cosmetic rather than radical, concentrating on reductions in cost and increases in stability. But now we live in a digital age. Digital processing has long been established in control desks and, for sending information from desk to dimmer, a single digitally multiplexed screened twin cable has replaced the old multicores with their separate wire for each channel. The latest dimmers have microprocessors (similar types to those used in motor cars for efficient engine management) which control their output by digital calculation. The traditional top and bottom adjustments are redundant: stability is independent of the ravages of temperature and time. Most of the many benefits which result from having a computing capability in the dimmer are too detailed for the scope of this discussion, but there is one which should be noted as something of a breakthrough.

Dimmers have fallen behind desks in ability to monitor their own performance and diagnose any faults. Before dimming became digital it was difficult to provide an indication of whether a lamp has blown or a plug been kicked out. Now it is possible to display an indication in the control room of whether the output from a dimmer is reaching the instrument – and thus alert the operator to a blown lamp or kicked out plug.

Integral Dimmers

There would seem to be a case in certain circumstances for considering a thyristor dimmer placed inside a conventional halogen lamped instrument rather than at a central distribution point. This method could well simplify rigging, particularly for one-night-stands, and experiments are taking place.

4
Rigging and wiring

We have now established aims in lighting, and surveyed the basic types of equipment which are available to convert these aims into reality. Before discussing the use of the equipment to achieve our aims, let us look at the methods of mounting the instruments (*rigging*) and supplying them with electricity (*wiring*).

RIGGING

The design of all UK lighting instruments includes a bolt and wing nut for rigging. For lighter instruments this bolt has an M.10 thread and for heavier types it is M.12. Equipment made before this metric standard was adopted in the early 1980s use a ³⁄₈in or ¹⁄₂in whitworth thread. All lights are designed to hang vertically from this bolt, and any other angle may shorten the lamp life considerably, even reducing it from several hours to a few minutes. This is because projection lamps are designed to burn on a certain axis and spotlights are designed, not merely to use the lamp within its limits, but to keep the lamp case temperature to a minimum by an accurate flow of convection air currents.

The most convenient fixing is standard scaffolding tube (48mm external diameter) and, to ensure that the lamp hangs at the correct attitude, this scaffolding should be horizontal or vertical. Horizontal scaffold tubes are known as *bars* (*pipes* in North America) while verticals are *booms*. Instruments are hung from bars by *hook clamps* and bracketed from booms by *boom arms*. Brackets may be used for direct wall fixing but are very limiting as they provide only a series of fixed positions. Some swivel models are torture to adjust from the top of a ladder. The restrictions imposed by brackets apply particularly to positions in the auditorium: if basic provision is made with scaffolding-size bars, there is flexibility for getting lights into the most suitable positions for each production. To solve a particularly knotty problem, there is always the possibility of attaching an extra temporary short length of bar by means of

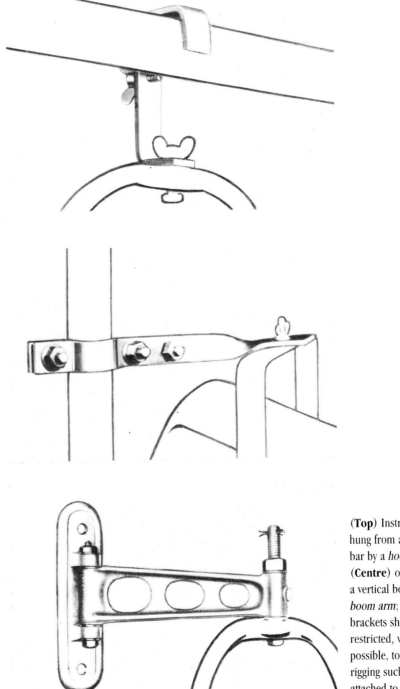

(**Top**) Instruments are hung from a horizontal bar by a *hook clamp*; (**Centre**) or hung from a vertical boom by a *boom arm*; (**Bottom**) brackets should be restricted, where possible, to temporary rigging such as spots attached to scenery timbers.

standard scaffolding clamps. Very few landlords take kindly to temporary brackets being screwed to their walls.

When mounting on floor stands, wing nuts are replaced by *spigots* made in sizes to fit the standard hanging bolts.

Truss Rigging

When a long and/or heavily loaded single bar would have insufficient rigidity, lights are hung on trusses made from cross-braced scaffolding sized tubing.

Truss sections are used as an alternative to simple scaffolding pipes when extra rigidity is required (*Optikinetics Trilite* system.)

Productions are being staged increasingly in venues without traditional flying facilities. When there are few suspension points, or when there are none at all, the lighting rig has to be supported from floor level. To solve this problem the rock music industry has pioneered the development of complete rigs of trussing, strong and rigid yet lightweight, hoisted and supported totally from the floor.

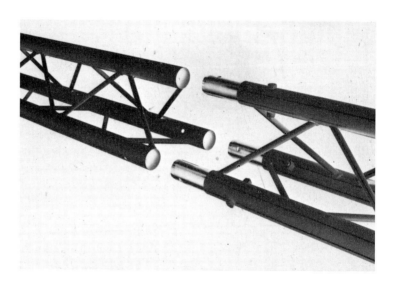

Rigging Safety

It is obvious that anything hanging above the actor or audience is a potential hazard. Modern lighting instruments are designed not to fall apart, and today's moulded lenses are most unlikely to crack and scatter broken glass. The dangers are human error: it is essential that anyone fixing or adjusting a light should take meticulous care to ensure that all fixing nuts are tight. As an additional precaution, each instrument should have a *safety chain*.

PERMANENT WIRING

There are two kinds of wiring in a stage installation: permanent
and temporary. Permanent wiring should always terminate in
sockets so that instruments can be removed easily for cleaning
and servicing. The standard British professional socket for stage
use on channels rated up to 2.4 kW is the 15 amp 3-round-pin
BESA. In smaller installations with channels rated at only 1 kW
the smaller 5 amp 3-round pin BESA is sometimes found, but
this complicates the use of rented and borrowed equipment.
Some of the most dangerous electrical situations that I have
seen on stages have arisen from plugs hastily changed in a spirit
of 'the show must go on'. The not too distant future is likely to
see a common standard throughout the EEC.

Plugs should not be of the fused type: fuse checking and replacement is a matter to be dealt with at ground level and at a
central position – not while groping about with one and a half
hands at the top of a ladder. Stage fusing is centralised at the
dimmers with either circuit breakers or fuse holders of the right
type and capacity being incorporated by all manufacturers in
their dimmer racks. Normally these fuseholders will accept
only the correct rating of fuse.

Because one dimmer often feeds more than one light, a
channel tends to be terminated in two adjacent sockets. Generally speaking, lights mounted in the auditorium (known as 'foh',
jargon for 'front-of-house') are moved less frequently than
those mounted on-stage. Therefore foh sockets can be
positioned close to the actual instrument position to reduce the
amount of flexible wiring between instrument and socket. On
stage, however, it is usually simpler and more adaptable to
place the sockets in blocks at the side of the stage, since the positioning of lighting equipment above the stage tends to be much
more flexible to meet the varying requirements of different productions. Most sockets are positioned at a high level to feed
lights hanging above the stage. It is usually convenient to have
most, but not all, of the sockets on one side of the stage and to
save money this is often the side nearest to the dimmers. Where
there is a choice, it is usual to opt for stage left. (The terms left
and right always refer to actors, *facing* their audience.) However, for maximum flexibility, it is useful to have some circuits
looped across to alternative sockets on the other side.

Bars can be obtained with cabling running inside scaffolding-
sized tube. The individual circuits are fed through holes in the
bar at intervals of about two feet. These bars are really only suit-

able for installations, or parts of installations, where the instrument mounting positions are absolutely constant, with virtually no flexibility required from one production to another.

Some sockets are required on both sides of the stage at low level for the convenient feeding of groundrows and stand equipment. Such floor equipment is often moved and plugged during performance scene changes. Traditionally, stage sockets have been positioned under the stage with access through small traps known as *dips*: this is often not worth the expense on small stages, particularly as traps are frequently made temporarily inaccessible by scenery. Many new stages have blocks of sockets mounted on the upstage and downstage walls. A continuous shallow trough runs up and downstage in the wings with a lid which lifts in sections enabling temporary cables to be run partly below stage level for safety.

The essential features of permanent wiring are:

(1) That it is well-planned – not merely for the way that a stage is being used now, but to allow flexibility for inevitable future development.

(2) That it complies with standard stage practice and is installed by qualified electrical contractors to the highest specifications in accordance with the appropriate regulations, national and local.

(3) That it is never, *but never*, interfered with. No matter how urgently desirable or necessary a re-arrangement of permanent wiring may seem, such alterations should only be undertaken by qualified electrical contractors working to the same practices, specifications and regulations as would apply to a new installation.

(4) That it is checked regularly by a qualified inspector.

Patching

On smaller stages, variations in rigging are dealt with by running temporary cable from the lights to the socket outlets around the stage. On a small stage such temporary cable runs will be relatively short, but problems arise in a large theatre – particularly an adaptable one with possibilities of alternative staging arrangements such as varying degrees of thrust. Under these conditions, it is worth considering a *patching* system which places the equivalent of a sort of telephone exchange between the dimmers and a larger number of socket positions. In its simplest form, this can be merely the termination of permanent wiring in a series of short flexible tails which are plugged into dimmer sockets as required; or it can be a quite sophisticated frame of interconnecting *jack*-plugs and *jill*-sockets. For the very biggest stages, particularly those playing in repertoire, it is becoming increasingly economical to install a dimmer for every single one of a very large number of sockets and to soft patch those required for a particular production to the desk via its microprocessor – that is, a sort of electronic telephone exchange is placed between dimmers and desk, rather than a manual one between dimmers and sockets. Soft patching is also being increasingly recognised as a timesaver for touring companies since it allows each instrument to have the same channel number in each theatre on the tour. Whatever the means, the essence of patching is that it reduces the amount of temporary wiring required for each production by providing a means of quick and easy central selection of the particular socket outlets which are geographically appropriate.

TEMPORARY WIRING

If the permanent wiring has been installed properly, temporary additions in flexible cable can be made by anyone with some sound electrical common sense. It is usual to use rubber-clad plugs and sockets to withstand the occasional knocks and drops that are inevitable in stage working. All cable should be amply rated for the maximum electrical load that is likely to be carried. It is essential that:

(1) Live, Neutral and Earth are firmly attached to the correct terminals.
(2) The cable is firmly clamped by the cable grip at the point where it enters the plug or socket so that no strain whatsoever is placed on the individual wire connections.
(3) The cable is run neatly, without sharp bends, and clear of direct heat from the lights. Cable should be anchored at intervals with sticky plastic tape to prevent strain being placed on the plug and socket connections.
(4) Before each use, the cable is inspected to check that;
    (a) there are no cuts or nicks in the outer protective sheathing,
    (b) all screws on the plugs and sockets are tight.
If there is the slightest doubt, the plug or socket should be opened for inspection.

All this is, in fact, the common sense that should be applied to the installation of all domestic appliances. It must be emphasised again and again that the main danger on a stage is cutting corners in safety precautions in a spirit of 'the show must go on'. This corner cutting is rarely intentional. It arises out of mental concentration on what appears to be the overwhelmingly impossible problems of getting the show on in the inadequate time available. This need to beat the clock means that critical work is done under conditions of physical and mental tiredness. The only method is constant safety checking and double checking.

ELECTRICAL PHASING

In some countries, including Britain, regulations require that a distance of six feet be maintained between equipment on separate phases of the electrical supply. This is a safety precaution because of the larger voltages that exist between phases. Where these rules apply, it is customary to try to have at least all on-stage lighting on the same phase. This is often difficult on small stages and becomes impossible with larger installations. The usual custom is to wire the overhead equipment to a different phase from the equipment at stage level. Where this is done, the phases should be clearly marked on the socket outlet boxes, and care should be taken to warn all personnel of the possible dangers of running flys to stage and *vice versa*.

If a patch panel is installed, the jill-sockets should be marked with the phase of their particular dimmer supply, and the jack-plugs with the phase of their particular geographical position on the stage. The clearest and simplest method is probably by colour coding: patching identical colours will then indicate and ensure correct patching.

5
Direction and focus

The real crunch in lighting is where we place the lights, what we point them at and how we adjust their beams. If we have not positioned, pointed and focused correctly, the most virtuoso performance on the most elaborate control board will not make the whole greater than the sum of its parts. It is the placing and pointing decisions that are the creative part of realising a lighting concept. The actual focusing – the adjusting of beams – is more a matter of technique.

LIGHTING THE ACTOR

Because they have to stand out from their background, actors are normally lit to a brighter level than scenery. In an ideal world, actors and scenery would be lit completely independently. No actor light would hit the scenery and no scenery light would hit the actors. Except in very occasional circumstances on the largest of stages, such a completely controlled situation is just not practical. The nearest we can get to this ideal is to keep any actor light falling on the scenery to a minimum. The setting is then mainly lit by the reflected light bouncing off the floor and furnishings, plus some instruments used to stress the sculptural quality of the scenic pieces and highlight appropriate features.

Let us consider the effect on the actor of light from various directions. There are three variables:
(1) The effect on the actor
(2) The area of stage lit
(3) The shadow cast.

Front Light

Consider an actor standing still and facing the audience (A). Light from above, absolutely vertically downwards. The eyes will be dark sockets, the nose aglow and causing the mouth to lie in shadow. There will be virtually no shadow on the floor and only a very small area of the stage will be lit: an area that need be no larger than the circumference of the actor's widest part – chest, waist, or hips depending on physique. A light that is very selective, dramatic in its modelling, but doing nothing to let the audience see the actor's principal means of projection: eyes and teeth.

Now move that light a little forward of the actor (B). It will start to reach the eyes and mouth (provided that she keeps her chin up and is not defeated by a hat brim!). The area lit and the shadow cast will start to extend upstage behind the actor.

As the light comes lower from the front (C), the actor's eyes and teeth become more visible. But the lit area extends further upstage, reducing selectivity and increasing the likelihood of the actor's shadow hitting the scenery. This shadow will climb increasingly up the scenery as the direction of the light is lowered. When the light reaches horizontal (D), eyes and teeth will be fully lit and the shadow will be the same height as the

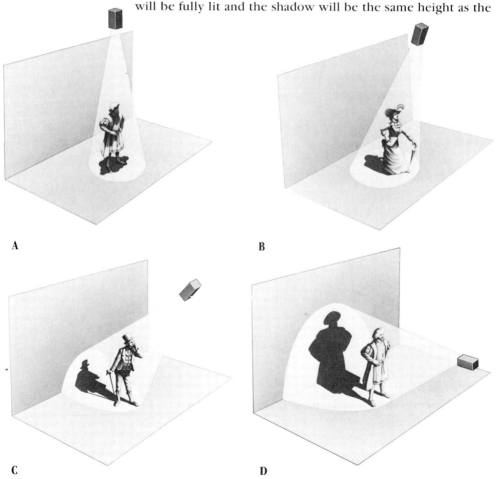

A

B

C

D

actor. The area selected by the light will be a corridor which is as narrow as the actor's width but extends the full depth of the acting area because the light will go on and on until it hits either a piece of scenery or the back wall of the stage. This is all, of course, for an actor standing still: moving to the left or right will require the corridor width to increase to accommodate the extent of these movements. Furthermore, although facial visibility has improved, its quality has decreased: whereas the vertical light was sculptural, the horizontal light is flattening. Therefore the nose seems not to protrude and the eyes not to recede. So there seems to be an identifiable compromise: low enough for eyes and teeth, yet high enough to avoid excessive flattening and to restrict the area of lit floor and the extent of the shadows. Perhaps somewhere around 30°–60°? Degrees from the horizontal or vertical? Doesn't matter since 30° and 60° are interchangeable. Just where we position the spot within this arc will depend upon just how tight an area we need to select. The compromise will involve choices between relative visibility, sculptural modelling, shadows and selectivity. Whatever we choose, the light inevitably will tend to be flattening rather than flattering.

Side Light

Having discussed light in the frontal plane, let us now consider side light – light in a plane at 90° to the front light. What happens when we move our vertical downlight to the side of the actor rather than to the front (E)? As the angle moves down, the actor's face and body become increasingly sculpted. A little light gets under the eyebrows and into the eyes, while rather more gets under the nose and into the mouth. Also, as the light-

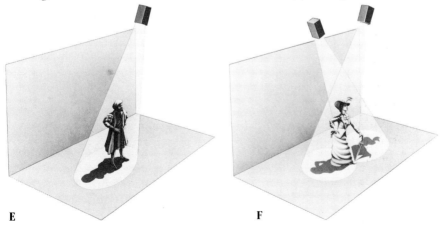

E   F

ing angle becomes lower, the area lit and the actor's shadow lengthens across the stage. If the actor is facing out front, lights will be required from both sides (F) in order to illuminate both sides of the face – although there will tend to be a central dark line where the beams meet down the centre of the face. The two lights automatically produce two shadows. So, with side lighting we note that modelling and visibility increase, while selectivity decreases, as the angle comes down from the vertical (G). When the angle becomes horizontal (H), there will be a complete light corridor across the stage. It will be actor high but its depth, up and downstage, will be dependent on the requirements of actor movement. Compromise is again likely to lead us somewhere into a zone of 30°–60°, but the precise range will depend on several factors arising from the production's re-

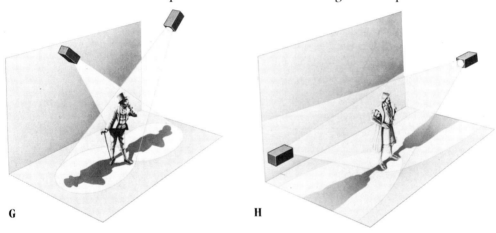

G   H

quirements. How tightly selected need the areas be? Is there a lot of movement to be sculpted? (Dancers, almost by definition, tend to project more with their bodies than do actors.) How will the scene design accept shadows? (If there are on/off flats, their angles can be cheated imperceptibly so that they do not catch shadows but lose them in the bays between the wings. If there are walls running up and downstage, actor high shadows are likely to prove unacceptable, although scenic colour and texture might permit a more acceptable level of tolerance.)

Back Light

A light from behind the actor (J) will not illuminate the face, but it helps to enhance stage depth by separating actor from scenery by creating a haze between them. The highlights on the head and shoulders also help to sculpt the actor. The shadow is cast forward and this helps with area selection on the stage floor and, since lighting does not fall on the face, strongly atmospheric colours may be used.

Light from Below

Light from below horizontal (K) projects an actor shadow that looms above the actor as she moves forwards and away from the light source. When this is the only direction, or the predominant direction, from which the light comes, the effect on the face is not at all natural. But a little light from below, often just reflected light, can help to soften the inevitable harshness of light from above. Such reflected light, however, will be very unselective.

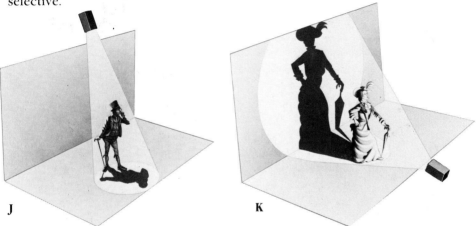

J   K

The Compromise

This exploration of possible lighting angles suggests that there is no ideal position for a single light. Front angles are strong on visibility, side angles on sculptural modelling. High angles are more selective than lower ones which open up the area of stage lit and lengthen the actor shadows. So we must seek a compromise which will allow the actor to be lit for maximum visibility and maximum modelling, yet with minimum shadow, plus, for many productions, the selection of as tight an area as possible. The standard method is to use a pair of lights (L) from directions which compromise between the front and side extremes: light coming from the front of the actor (for visibility) but offset to the side (to help modelling). Mounted high enough to keep the shadows short enough for the actor to dominate them, yet low enough for the light to get into the eye

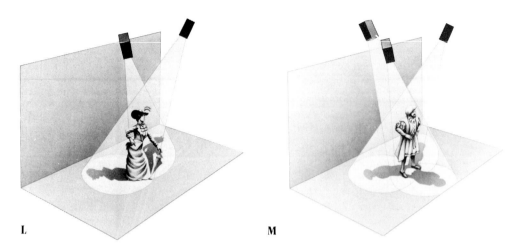

L   M

sockets (if the eyebrows are not too bushy or the hat brim too wide) and into the mouth with its all important teeth (if the nose be reasonably restrained in its projection).

A crossed pair of lights used in this way has been the standard approach for at least sixty years – it was first described by Stanley McCandless in his 1932 *A Method of Lighting the Stage*. The main addition since then has been backlight to emphasise the depth of the scene and generally enhance the 'look' of the actor. During earlier phases in the development of lighting, the first priority had to be to get enough plain illumination followed by modelling and area control. On considerations of cost-effectiveness, backlight had to come well down the list. However if light is to be the actor's environment on the stage as it is in nature, that light must come from all around. Accordingly we now give a high priority to backlight (M), even when equipment is short.

The vertical angle of the backlight is not critical: it need only be 20° or so beyond the vertical and indeed, in many tightly hung rigs, the backlight is virtually a downlight. Whether it is offset to the side is largely dependent on whether it is necessary and desirable to introduce a directional key as part of the motivational concept of a particular lighting picture.

Therefore the standard method has become to light each acting area with spots from *three primary angles*: a pair (one from each side) from the front plus one from behind. We may mix in a little from other spots at front and sides, but these are *secondary angles* often used as washes to include several areas within their focus settings – and added only into the bigger scenes.

An Alternative

The problem with the three angle system is threefold. Firstly, diagonal shadows are thrown in two contrasting directions away from the actor, making it difficult to control the light on the set. Secondly, they light an area of stage floor considerably in excess of the acting area provided with good face lighting – and that area of lit floor does not correspond with the area above it where faces are lit. Thirdly, and probably most important, once the angles have been chosen, the compromise between visibility and modelling is fixed. The balance between visibility and modelling is one of the most important features of designed lighting. Indeed it is such a fundamental part of the lighting designer's 'palette' that perhaps we ought to aim to have separate angles (from separate instruments on separate dimmers) for frontal visibility and side modelling.

There is an increasing tendency to light with *four primary angles* with a separation of 90° between them. With this method, visibility comes from the front while a backlight helps to remove the flatness (N). If we need to select a tightly controlled upstage/downstage corridor without side spillage, this provides an acceptable light. However, side lights are normally added for modelling (O) and, although they will spread the lit area, they can be at quite steep angles since they do not make a major contribution to visibility. By balancing the side against the front, we can vary the relative stress placed on visibility and modelling during the progress of the play. We may also add a bit from side-front angles but these are *secondary angles* used only when we can afford to widen out the selected area for big scenes. By using *tertiary angles* for backlight, we have the possibility of giving the lighting a directional motivation.

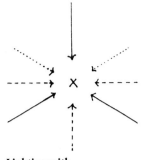

Lighting with three lamps

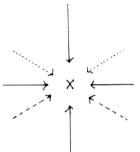

Lighting with four lamps

──────⟶ Primary angles

── ── ── ⟶ Secondary angles

············⟶ Tertiary angles

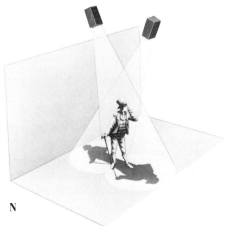

N

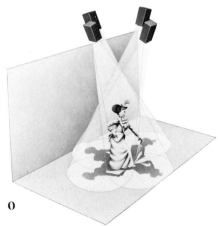

O

Light from front

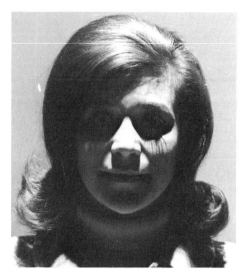

Light from above

Light from below

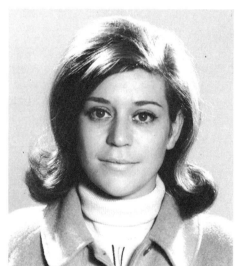

Balanced light

SIMPLICITY

It is becoming obvious from this discussion that having a completely controlled situation will require a large series of lights on the actor from various angles. This is why some professional productions have very large lighting rigs. *And so a timely word of warning.* A large palette of lights becomes frighteningly difficult to use – and takes a frightening amount of time to balance. The cleanest lighting is often the simplest, and so we need to set out with positive aims and try to achieve these aims with the minimum of equipment.

Some very exciting lighting may be achieved by using only two or three very powerful sources from very carefully selected positions. Perhaps a discharge lamped film studio light through a window, or parlamp light curtains bouncing off a white glazed floor. For this to succeed some action may have to be rather carefully choreographed to position the actors in the most advantageous positions. A few discreet cheat sources may be added to boost the natural reflections of the major sources. But this should be done with the greatest care in order to avoid escalation into a big rig in which the positive advantage of a few major intense sources will be lost.

PRACTICALITIES OF POSITIONING

We shall be returning to these matters of design in later chapters but meanwhile, on the basis of that old cliché 'one lamp in the right place is worth untold lamps in the wrong place', let us consider the practicalities of placing our lighting instruments in the positions that seem theoretically ideal. This problem divides itself into two situations: the auditorium and the stage. In the auditorium, architecture is the major influence on availability of positions which therefore tend to remain the same from one production to the next. On stage there is a conflict of interests between positions for scenery and lighting: therefore a new compromise usually needs to be sought for each production.

Auditorium Positions

Auditoria fall into two categories: those built before the development of modern stage lighting and those built since. In theory, those built in, say, the last thirty to fifty years should include adequate provision for mounting spotlights in good, if not always totally ideal, positions. Alas, this is not always so. It is only since perhaps the early 1970s that we have been able to take this for granted in new professional theatres. And for new community and school halls, decent lighting positions still may not be assumed.

Modern theatre architecture is at great pains not to stress the proscenium arch. To avoid a framing effect, the proscenium is formed by the natural termination of the ceiling and side

Ceiling bridges and wall slots incorporated into the architecture of a modern auditorium provide accessible lighting positions. (*Theatr Clwyd, Mold.*)

walls. In such a structure it is relatively easy to form unobtrusive horizontal lighting positions within the ceiling and vertical ones in the side walls. Ceiling positions should run the entire width of the auditorium, with the lights mounted on access bridges where electricians can stand comfortably to focus with a clear view of the stage. Side slots should, as far as possible, extend the full height of the wall. They normally need to terminate above audience head height: this is not a problem since, as we have noted, the majority of lighting angles should be considerably above the horizontal. The boom in a wall slot should have a permanent access ladder and/or a series of platforms. If there is an apron stage thrusting through the proscenium, or if the orchestra pit is likely to be adapted to such use, a third bridge (certainly) and third pair of slots (desirable) will be required. In the pursuit of intimacy, current theatre architecture tends to favour a return to the older practice of hanging audience on the side walls in boxes or by extending the galleries along the side walls in what has become known as courtyard format. This requires considerable ingenuity in providing side foh lighting positions.

In older theatres with a formal proscenium arch, the ceiling is normally unsuitable for lighting positions, being both too high and too much of a decorative feature. However the fronts of circles make possible hanging positions with the highest gallery normally providing a good face angle. This is rarely good in cinematic theatres built between the wars and having only one low circle. Side positions are difficult in old theatres: boxes can be used but their view of the stage is usually quite restricted. In recent years it has become customary to erect booms almost on the proscenium arch itself and to hang a bar, known as an 'advance bar', from the auditorium ceiling close to the top of the proscenium – usually over the orchestra pit or the first row of stalls seating. While such positions are excellent for lighting, they hardly enhance a beautiful old auditorium. Some years ago, when only a few foh spots were normal, it was usual to conceal them in fibrous plaster boxes matching the auditorium decor. However, growth in size of lighting rigs now results in old theatres being festooned with lighting. This solution is generally accepted, supported by a sizable school of thought that likes the technology to be exposed. (My own position is that while I acknowledge that there are production styles which require all to be revealed, there are certainly many others which benefit from the means of magic being masked.)

In multi-purpose halls, provision for foh lighting should be made by fixing scaffolding (not brackets) from the ceiling and on the side walls. Ladders of correct type and height should always be available for access.

Backstage Positions

Apart from the 'No 1 Spot Bar' position always required immediately behind the proscenium arch, lighting designers like to be able to keep an open mind about where the other lighting bars should be hung. However, theatres with fast changeovers between productions require some sort of permanent rig and so spot bars tend to be positioned approximately every eight feet. This enables reasonably constant angles to be maintained on actors throughout the depth of the stage. Each spot bar has the possibility of fulfilling two basic functions: providing a sculpting light for actors standing underneath it and a face light for those upstage of it. This is discussed in later chapters. In central European theatres presenting a repertoire with extensive daily changeovers between daytime rehearsals and different productions each evening, there is a bridge (or vertical stack of three bridges) and a pair of lighting towers immediately behind the proscenium: these give immediate access to all lights which can even be refocused during quick scene changes in the performance.

Focusing with back to light

Side lighting positions are almost totally variable, being dependent upon the structure of the scenery, particularly gaps in the side masking. The only feasible position for permanent booms is immediately adjacent to the proscenium. Booms and ladders upstage of this are positioned as required for each production, although some theatres have ladders mounted in heavy duty sliding tracks under the fly galleries, allowing their positions to be moved easily. Low level lights, particularly for dance, may be mounted on stands or castored trucks.

FOCUSING

Having placed the lighting instruments in the selected positions, they have to be adjusted. This process of angling the spotlights and adjusting their beams is sometimes called *setting* or more usually *focusing*.

When we focus a light on an actor position, our prime concern is to check that the light covers all the area in which we expect the actor to be lit by that particular instrument. I find that the only practical way to do this is to move around personally in the beam and check that the light does hit me. And, to save my eyes, I turn my back to the light and watch my shadow. If there is a full shadow of me plus hand (to allow for the fact that all actors in my shows seem to be seven foot tall), I am lit. This method allows me to check the secondary point of concern in focusing a light: the mess that the beam is making after it has hit the actor.

The trouble with beams of light is that you cannot control their length. You can cut bits out of the their sides with shutters, and you can cut bits out of their middles with gobos, but you cannot cut a bit off the end of the beam. Most of our lighting is focused on the actors and it would be marvellous if we could chop off the beams after they have passed the actors and before they hit the scenery. But the light beam passes resolutely on until it hits the scenery with a nasty splodge, often drawing audience attention away from the very actor whom it was designed to illuminate.

What can we do about this problem? It is not much good focusing another light on to the scenery to smooth out the splodge, for the scenery will then become so bright that the actor in front of it will darken into silhouette. Up a point on the actor and the shadow again becomes predominant. Compensating with a point more on the scenery and the actor is back into silhouette, escalating in no time at all into the brightest darkspot on the stage.

Much of the putting and pointing of lights is concerned with finding ways of lighting the actor so that the end of the beam falls where it will do little damage: off-stage or on the floor, rather than on a prominent bit of scenery. But this can breed a very large rig which often introduces more lighting problems than it solves – apart from requiring an excess of money, time and space.

So what can we do about the actor light that just has to fall on the scenery whether we like it or not? The technique is *clean focusing* and consists principally of paying adequate attention to the edges of the beam. There are two inescapable rules here (how nice to find an occasional rule in such a subjective business as stage lighting!):

(1) Soft edges are less noticeable than hard.
(2) Any beam edges are less noticeable if they coincide with an architectural edge.

The easy route to soft edges is using a fresnel spot but, in providing a soft-edge, the fresnel by its very nature throws out an embarrassing amount of scatter light close to the lens. This scatter light is particularly unwelcome if we are using borders. Light should be kept completely away from neutral borders, while painted borders need a carefully balanced light. Our aim is to make the audience look down onto the action, not up at the masking arrangements. PC lens spots produce much less scatter but there is less margin for error when overlapping their beams in a smooth join. Soft edges with virtually no scatter light can be produced by profile spots but this takes valuable time which is in short supply in the schedules of most productions (but see note on diffusers below). I would therefore advocate, when short of time or experience (and particularly when short of both!) the use of PCs or fresnels for actor lighting from the on-stage lighting positions, simply because mistakes don't show – or at least don't show so much.

However, with the exception of micro-mini stages, the scatter and lack of throw from a fresnel makes it unsuitable for use in the auditorium: from this position we normally need a profile spot. It is these foh spots which cause the worst mess on the scenery as a result of the relatively flat lighting angle which auditorium architecture often makes inevitable. So, like it or not, we just have to find time to focus the foh with soft precision. In a permanent installation, the foh spots usually do a similar job in most productions and so they can be permanently softened. The main problems arise when foh have to be rigged specially for each show.

Diffusers

A possible solution to quick, easy softening is the use of diffusers which have become more versatile in recent years. 'Frost' filters have always been available but they produce a heavy softening compared with the range of subtle diffusion filters now manufactured. Hard focusing of a profile spot is simple and fast – and Rosco 119 or the even more subtle

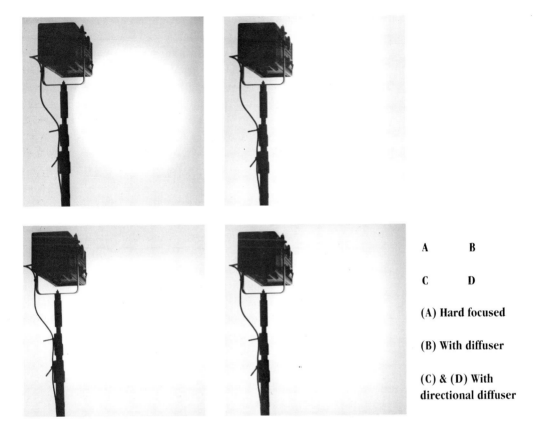

A   B

C   D

(A) Hard focused

(B) With diffuser

(C) & (D) With directional diffuser

Rosco 164 will soften the whole beam, including its edge without creating any significant spill.

Other relatively new diffusers which have rapidly become indispensable are the directional types known as 'silks' (e.g. Rosco 104 and 160). While diffusing the light this also stretches it out in one plane: by framing the filter at the appropriate angle we can elongate the light in whichever direction we choose. A directional diffuser is particularly useful when working with a small amount of equipment but it can also be very useful for generally tidying up the lighting 'look'.

Even after careful focusing, however, we are still left with an edge, albeit a soft one. To make this edge seem natural, it is helpful to line it up with an architectural feature of the scenery – door frames, picture frames, etc., are naturals on a realistic set.

Gobos

So much for the edge of the beam. What about the inside of the beam? Textured surfaces tend to be less obtrusive than flat surfaces under light. Scenic surfaces are easy to texture: indeed some scene designers have a habit of rushing at their sets with handfuls of gunge and spatters of vandyke brown as soon as I start to light. But it is interesting to texture the light itself. The obvious way is to use a gobo with irregular holes to produce the quality of light that falls through trees. I have even used such break-up texturing very, very softly inside a *Who's for Tennis* interior setting without anyone muttering about trees.

POSTSCRIPT

If my life in lighting has had any revelations, I think it is the discovery that the better I focus the lamps, the fewer the cues I need. I can remember shows where half the cues consisted of fiddling with levels of lights which were ugly on the scenery and had to be up when the actors were in that area and down when they were elsewhere. I can remember hours wasted in the still watches of the night, delicately balancing dimmer levels to avoid hardness on the scenery – only to take it all up a couple of points next morning when we had actors. I still do it.

There is an old board operator's saying: 'If you do it slowly and smoothly enough, you can get away with murder'. The equivalent for focusing is: 'If you set it softly enough . . . '.

And, returning to the theme of simplicity, there is no point in indulging in a large expensive multi-instrument lighting rig unless adequate time is available for focusing.

Remote-controlled Spotlights

The development of sophisticated instruments with remote operation and memorising of focus adjustments will obviously have a considerable bearing on future lighting rigs. These spots, however, do not change the need for precise selection of hanging position to allow the light to strike actor or scenery at the most appropriate angle. Once the spotlight has been hung in its fixed position, focus adjustments need no access and so it is easy to refine beam precision and quality throughout the rehearsal period.

But reduction in the number of instruments in a rig can only be achieved by refocusing when an instrument is not in use and when the hanging position of the instrument is appropriate. Full flexibility awaits the development of spotlights which travel along lighting bars!

6
Colour

Of all the variables in stage lighting, *colour* is probably the most difficult to control. There is no problem in colouring a single beam, but it is not easy to predict the total additive effect of mixing several coloured beams.

Colour filters are often referred to colloquially as *gels*, a shortening of the word 'gelatine' from which filters were formerly made. Gelatine, however, is a fire-risk and has disappeared into theatrical history along with such other colouring devices as tinted glass and lacquer.

All colour filtering is now by non-inflammable flexible plastic material manufactured in sheet or roll form under varying trade names. Special types of filter are designed to withstand the intensity of the newer light sources: such filters are particularly useful for parcans and linear floods, although with the general increase in lamp efficiency, they are finding increasing favour as the standard filter material on professional stages.

The colour control of a single light is relatively easy: we select a filter and Hey Presto! Well, not quite Hey Presto, because, as a lamp is dimmed, its filament grows progressively redder and the light becomes warmer. Pale tints will therefore noticeably change colour as the light dims, and a pale steel can become quite rosy. This is not necessarily a disadvantage for it can be very useful at times for a scene to become warmer as the brightness is reduced. But it is a factor that has to be taken into account when working with colour filters.

The colour from a single light will also depend on the type of lamp. The difference between tungsten and tungsten-halogen has turned out to be less worrying than expected and can almost be ignored for most work. But the difference between the same filter with an incandescent lamp and with a discharge lamp (such as a CSI) can be quite startling due to the bluer light emitted by the discharge source.

FILTERING COLOUR

When we put a filter in front of a spotlight we feel as if we are adding colour to that light. 'Put a blue in' we say, as if we were adding blue. But 'Take out all colours except blue' would be a more accurate request. Certainly for a deeply saturated blue. For a paler blue we might say 'Take out all colours except all the blue, some of the green and a trace of everything else.' Or for a different pale blue tint 'Leave only all the blue, some of the red and a bit of everything else.' It is important to remember that when we place a filter in front of a light we are taking colour away — filtering it out. Filtering emphasises certain colours in the spectrum by removing the rest.

Unfiltered light (usually called 'open white') contains all the colours in the spectrum (or of the rainbow if you prefer a more romantic approach!). By passing this light through a filter, we are not colouring the light, but are removing (i.e. filtering out) the other colours. Thus a deep red primary filter will remove everything except the red part of the spectrum: that is, it will let through only the red. A paler red filter will let through all the red and some of the other colours. A pale rosy tint will let through all the red and quite a lot of the other colours.

This ability of pale filters to let through a certain amount of the other colours is very important. Materials, whether painted scenic canvas, dyed costume fabric, actor flesh, or whatever, will only respond sympathetically to light under one condition: in the material there must be some pigment of the same basic colour as the light. If a scene is painted completely in blue pigments, it is very difficult to get it to light to a satisfactory warm. Certainly, pouring lots of red rosy light on to such a scene will make it appear sort of warm: but it will be a colour response with no life. For a vibrant response, there must be some warm pigment present. This warm pigment need not be obtrusive: it can be just a little spatter which will only respond when there are warm tints in the light. Therefore, scene painting with a built-up texture of superimposed pigment will tend to respond well to colour variations in the light. Similarly, costumes usually respond better when the material texture is shot with traces of several pigments. Because pale filters let through a proportion of all colours, there will always be some sort of response from all pigments in set and costumes when paler tinted light is used. It need hardly be pointed out that flesh tones, particularly an actor's face, only look well in the palest tints.

The more a filter removes colours from the light, the more that filter will emphasise the pigments which respond to the colours remaining in the filtered light. However the use of increasingly deep filters, while leading to increasingly positive colour statements, is also likely to produce a deadening of the visual effect due to any lesser pigments which may be present being starved of their colours in the light. Thus the paler tints are generally the most sympathetic filters since, in addition to passing all of their particular colour, they pass varying amounts of the remainder of the spectrum.

COLOUR MIXING

The major difficulty of colour control is predicting just what colour will result from the addition of the several colour beams hitting a particular part of the stage from a series of angles.

Light mixing works rather differently from paint mixing. Mix assorted paint pigments together and you will gradually move towards black: mix the three primaries and you will actually get black. However, if you mix assorted light beams together, you will move towards white and if you add the lighting primaries together, you will get white light. This is *additive* colour mixing of light.

On the other hand, the mixing of filters rather than the resultant light, works in a *subtractive* way. Mixing assorted filters in front of one instrument will gradually move its light towards black (i.e. no light). Place the three primary filters in front of the same instrument and you will get no light.

CHOOSING COLOUR

Colour choice, like everything else, stems from decisions about production *style*. How are we going to use colour in a particular production? Are we going to use it at all? Is it going to be a white light show where we try to achieve our aims in terms of direction and intensity alone? Or is it going to be a pure white show using only variations in direction? Or perhaps a whiter than white show where there is no variation in any of the controllable variables?

The simplest motive for using coloured light on the stage is to enhance the look of the scenery, costumes and actors. This could be, for example, just a straightforward warming to provide a sympathetic rosy cosy glow for a comedy. Or adding the delicate grey steels which provided Brecht with his clear white light. (Unfiltered open white light being rather warm, Brecht, like the detergent manufacturers, adopted the traditional laundry technology of the blue bag which makes whites whiter than white.)

However, light is usually coloured to provide a means of not only establishing an atmosphere but controlling that atmosphere during the performance. This is done by mixing colours: perhaps the most classic case is the double-covering of acting areas in a play with two sets of spotlights, one coloured cool and the other warm, so that the emotional toning of the scene can be varied as the drama unfolds.

The response of the human eye and brain tend to be relative. In the first few moments of the performance, we establish our colour palette. If we establish cool and warm as being very slight digressions to either side of neutral white, then very soon the audience perception will adjust to this subtle difference. Alternatively if we establish quite heavy saturated contrasts in the opening minutes, this will set the scale of audience response and they will not react to subtle differences in colour tone.

If we decide on colour, is it variations of subtle tints? Or slam-bam-wham contrasts of saturated primaries? Or shall we use tints for the realistic scenes and move into contrasts for a dream sequence? Does cool/warm mean sad/happy? Or does it mean morning/evening? Or a bit of both? Or what? And so on: the first decision must be to determine what role colour will play in the production style.

Having decided this, the next stage is to choose a group of colours from the available ranges. Or if there is nothing that takes your fancy, concoct a subtractive mixture by putting two filters in the same frame. In early attempts at using colour, it is probably better to avoid subtractive mixing of two filters as much as possible: keep the number of variables to a minimum. Even very experienced lighting designers are reluctant to use two filters in the same frame, if only because they fade and burn out much faster.

Choose a *small* group of filters. Have just a couple of blues, a couple of pinks – or perhaps three. Certainly not a different colour for each and every instrument in the rig. Select the ones to which the set and costumes will respond. If the set has greeny-blue pigments, then choose greeny-blues for your cools. If the set blues are warm and purply, then that is the clue to the cool filter choice.

For the face lights in a play we might choose a pair of tints which will mix to provide a subtle range from a palest cool steel through neutral to a slightly warm golden rose. Whereas, for the atmospheric sculptural washes in a musical, we might opt for a range of middle saturation pink, blue and amber which will offer several quite colourful combinations yet also add up to a near-white neutral.

Filter manufacturers issue sample books with pieces of the actual filter. Hold the filter up to the light and study the colour of the light coming through. Shine coloured light from a spot (or even a pocket torch) on to the design, paint, or fabric and note the response.

Colour filters are known by numbers which rarely run in logical sequence. Nor is there much correspondence between the numbers of one manufacturer and another. Rumour has it that an international committee debated, at regular intervals for several years, the desirability of a universal numbering system for colour filters: they are reported to have given up on discovering that a nine digit number would be required to codify all the fine variations possible.

Neutrals are very important. Cinemoid 36 pale lavender, is the long running classic – as 'surprise pink' it revolutionised face lighting fifty years ago – but is now giving way to the wider range of lavenders. The particular joy of the neutral lavenders is that they tend to appear warm or cool according to whether other colours used on stage are predominantly warm or cool.

Correction filters are a useful addition to the ranges in recent years. These are very subtle tints which adjust the quality of the whiteness of the light, particularly for film and video which are very sensitive to 'colour temperature' – the inherent spectral colour of the various light sources which range from a high proportion of a red to high proportion of blue. Correction filters are particularly useful on the stage for adding that tiny pinch of blue which whitens a light and enhances its clarity.

LIGHTING DARKER SKINTONES

With darker skins some aspects of face lighting become more difficult while others become easier. Character projection in a theatre, dependent upon clear visibility of eyes and teeth, is helped considerably by their contrast with darker skin. But strong contrast between light clothing and dark skin can lose faces. Light absorbed rather than reflected by darker faces may seem a problem but absorbed light brings the bonus of an enriched quality to the skin and underlying bone structure. Maximising gains and minimising losses requires considerable liaison with costume and scene designers, and particular care with angles, textures and diffusion.

But the major area for care is filter choice. Blue is dangerous and green lethal, turning black skin to an unbecoming putty. Greens can be avoided but a palette without blue can be very limiting. The technique is to avoid green-blues and opt for those with high red content. Blue toning can be injected through heavy backlighting and careful sidelighting, with face neutrals selected from pale warm tints which can with advantage be stronger than is usual for white actors. Consequently with mixed casting a slight warming-up of white actors' make-up is usually necessary.

FILTER CHOICE

The key to successful filter choice is to devote as much concern to the colours which are being filtered out as to the colours which are being allowed to pass through. And so we try to choose filters which pass:

- a lot of the main colour that we wish to emphasise for atmospheric effect *plus*
- some of the other colours appropriate for stimulating a vibrant response.

A Process for Filter Choice

Like everything else in lighting, we have to decide the visual effect we want to achieve and then find a technical means of doing it. There is a progression through four key questions requiring answers . . . .

How is colour to be used in this production?

- To enhance the clarity of white light?
- To enhance the visual quality of the performers and their stage environment?
- To support the progress of the action with appropriate changes of atmosphere?
- Or?

How naturalistic will the colours be?

- Approximating to sunshine, moonshine, and practical lamps?
- Considerably heightened but still with a natural logic?
- Non-naturalistic?
- Or?

How contrasty will the colour palette be?

- Delicate tints?
- Strong tones?
- Heavy saturates?
- Or?

What are the colour characteristics of the set and costume designs?

- Do the cools tend towards blues with a greenish or reddish content?
- Do the warms tend towards pinks or golds?
- Or?

The Filter Palette

Such a questioning process enables a gradual narrowing of choice towards a relatively small palette of filters appropriate for the production. The selection of specific filter numbers is made with the aid of swatch books. Some manufacturers list the filters in their swatch books by their numbers, while others group them in colour families. Numerical listing assists filter management – finding, cutting and framing – because colours are always referred to by numbers, both on plans and in conversation. However when preparing a lighting design it is logical to choose first the colour, then the depth of saturation and finally the appropriate shade. Some people acquire swatches in pairs and rearrange one so that they have all filters filed by both systems.

DICHROIC FILTERS

Conventional colour filters work by absorption – that is, they hold back the unwanted colours in the spectrum. This process gradually destroys the filter whose life decreases rapidly in proportion to the increasing brightness from higher powered lights. Dichroic colour filters work by reflection – that is, they reflect away the unwanted colours. Although dichroic filters are very much more expensive than conventional filters, they have a much longer life. They can be washed with standard dishwashing detergent solutions and retain their colour stability for years. Their efficiency produces colours which are clearer, brighter and purer. This purity may be something of an Achilles heel: it is the impurities in traditional filters which often allow materials or flesh to respond, and so dichroics probably require rather more subtle mixing. Perhaps their most important advantage for theatre is their extreme resistance to heat.

It is this feature which enables them to be used by Vari-Lite to produce, by colour mixing, the wide, almost continuous, palette of colours. This heat resistance allows them not only to be positioned inside high powered discharge lamp spotlights but to be placed so close to the light source that small filters can be organised into colour mixing combinations.

We can therefore look forward in the coming century to choosing a precise colour for our lights, not by selecting a filter, but by 'painting' from the lighting control desk. In addition to selecting the intensity for each light in each cue, we shall have the option of choosing (and recording) any precise colour.

DIMENSIONAL COLOUR

The dimensional quality of light can be helped by using different filters from either side. A slight contrast in colour makes for an increased appearance of plasticity in the actor or object lit. As an alternative to colour variation, plasticity may be increased by a variation in intensity between one side and the other. Because intensity and colour interact, a variation in intensity will also produce a variation in colour. If we are not careful, the contrast between the two sides can become too great. Personally, I prefer to use a variation in intensity rather than a variation in colour. Such an intensity balance often grows naturally out of the way that the light direction is motivated by a key source. However when the style demands an even light from all sides, or when only a minimum amount of equipment is available, colour balance can be a useful way of increasing the dimensional plasticity of actor and scene.

THREE COLOUR MIXING – A HISTORICAL POSTSCRIPT

The mixing of the three primaries to get any desired shade has become an obsolescent, if not completely obsolete, method of using coloured light. For lighting actors, it is a technique belonging to a bygone era of covering the stage in a flat washing flood of light from battens and footlights. These batten and footlights were, ideally, in four colours: the three primaries of red, green, and blue to make the colour, plus white to control the dilution of that colour. For economy reasons, British theatres were often equipped with a three colour system without the white. Because this did not give a bright enough 'full-up', the green was usually removed to give a red, white and blue mix: this may have demonstrated the patriotism which was always a strong feature of Music Hall, but it produces a rather limited range of colour possibilities.

Despite the passing of this type of colour mixing, variety artists still write plots in terms of 'red stage', 'blue stage', 'colours', and 'full-up'. Red, blue and colours translate readily into 'warm', 'cool', and 'pretty', while the meaning of full-up is clear, even if it does not normally involve bringing every light to full.

Three colour mixing practice lasted longer on cycloramas where flooding is the natural method of lighting. Primaries or secondaries at top and bottom could produce any colours required but:

(1) it is a wasteful way of getting pale colours *and*

(2) over a long crossfade, it is difficult to keep the colours in balance as they move.

The starting and finishing states may be exact, but the cyclorama can pass through some rather devastating colours on the way. It has therefore become normal practice to choose for cyclorama lighting a series of filters closely related to the range of colours required for a particular production. As cycloramas are so often used in a sky sense, there are usually at least two blues in the three colour mix at the top and two blues in the three colour mix at the bottom. To give the cyclorama that extra illusion of depth which comes from a fine gradation of colour, the blues at the bottom should be subtly different tints from those chosen for the top.

COLOUR SUMMARISED

Inevitably, this is a limited and perhaps rather personal view of colour, offered only as a possible starting point for anyone about to make their own first experiments. The subject will continue to arise, of course, in later chapters discussing the lighting of different forms of production. Meanwhile a few filter tips:

• Never choose a filter by its name. Look at the colour of the light transmitted through it by holding a sample up to light. Or, better still, try the effect by shining filtered light on a piece of scenery or a piece of costume fabric or an actor's face. Or if the set and costumes will be executed faithfully from the designs, experiment with filtered light on the drawings and/or models. Our eye will tell us which filters produce the most sympathetic response.

• In choosing a filter, it is relatively easy to predict the effect of a single light. But prediction of the effect of several overlapping filtered lights is not so easy. Fortunately, however, their effect is additive. That is, while filtering a light removes parts of the spectrum, an overlap of various colours from various filtered lights will tend to put the spectrum together again. So overlapping of coloured lights moves us towards white neutrality.

- Blues with a green content can be rather unbecoming on actors faces: try to avoid in extended moonlight scenes.
- Lavenders are particularly sympathetic to faces. They also have the uniquely useful quality of not only blending well with other lights but taking on something of their character: thus they tend to appear warm or cold according to the predominant trend of the colouring of the other lights.
- The high intensity of the light produced by parcans allows use of the most heavily saturated filters. Note that the colour from a parcan will be considerably paler than the light from a conventional lens spotlight of similar wattage.
- If atmospheric colour is concentrated in the backlights and some of the side lighting, neutrals and pale tints can be used from the front to provide a visibility which is sympathetic to face and costume without diluting the overall colour effect.
- A slight colour differential between left and right sides can be used to help increase the sculptural modelling of an actor. This can be particularly valuable if dimmer sharing prevents directional keying by means of an intensity imbalance.
- When using break-up gobos to texture the light, slightly different gels in overlapping instruments will increase the depth of the texture. It also helps to use split-colours in each spot (two half size pieces of filter butt-joined in the frame).
- A floor which has a fine spatter of paint colour will be much more responsive to filtered light than a plain floor. This is particularly so with a black floor.
- It is difficult to light white cycloramas to a dark blue. Cyc cloths should have a very pale blue pigmentation which will aid response to blue light but not upset response to the rest of the spectrum.
- Use slightly different blues at the bottom of a sky to those at the top. Normally these should be slightly paler at the bottom but even when they have the same saturation, a difference in tint produces a gradation of colour up the cloth, enhancing the feeling of horizon and making the sky seem deeper and further away.
- Colour-changing mechanisms (wheels, scrollers etc) enable us to change the filter in a light, but they do not remove the need for double-covering with twinned lights for cross-fading and palette-mixing.

7
First steps in lighting design

We have discussed possible aims in lighting. We have looked at the hardware available for the production of controlled light on the stage. We have considered how this equipment can be mounted and how it can be fed with electricity. We have debated the effect of the direction of the light hitting an actor and the consequences of subtracting part of the spectrum with colour filters. We now come to the crunch: how do we bring all this together in the process of lighting design? Just how does one start when faced with a bare stage? Before discussing the formal process of lighting a show, let us look at the simplest possible situation. Starting with just one spot, one cable, and no dimmers, let us see how we can build up an effective use of, say, the first ten instruments. Apart from theoretical considerations, you may well have to light an actual show with such a restricted amount of equipment. I have certainly had to do it – and it can be fun.

We are moving away from objective scientific facts into an area of personal preference where no two individuals are likely to agree wholeheartedly. Theatre, like all art forms, includes a large measure of personal subjective response. There is no absolute objective standard for good lighting, just as there is no absolute objective standard for good acting. So, as this is a personal opinion, I shall write as if thinking aloud.

I hope that nobody has to start as low down the scale as step one, but if anyone does, there is only one light to acquire and one place to put it. The spot is a fresnel, and the position is centre in the auditorium ceiling. The distance of the spot from the stage will depend on the width of the acting area, and the beam angle of the spotlight. If we know two of these we can calculate the third. The simplest method is to draw the situation at a suitable scale such as ¼ inch to the foot (50:1 if you are metricated). Knowing the spread and beam throw, the required beam angle can be read off with a protractor. Or knowing the beam angle of an available spot (from the manufacturer's catalogue), the spread of light from any throw can be discovered. If no manufacturer's catalogue is available, use my

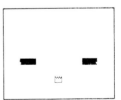

A

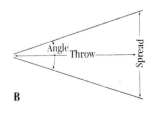

B

technique for getting to know equipment: when a new spotlight hits the market, I may often be seen assessing its throw by wandering around a theatre with the thing tucked under my arm, and a trailing cable creating havoc in my wake. But always remember that:

(1) most spotlights are less effective when used to their limits of maximum and minimum beam angle *and*

(2) all spotlights can be spotted down from their maximum but not flooded bigger than it.

So choose a slightly wider spread than your calculations suggest. Or, if you already have the spotlight, place it a little further away from the stage than seems theoretically correct.

However, the problem in placing spotlights in the auditorium is not so much one of deciding theoretically good positions but finding positions which are architecturally possible while being remotely suitable. In small halls, the problem is usually one of insufficient height. If the light hits the actors at a near horizontal angle it will have, to put it mildly, a flattening effect. When actors face the audience, their eyes will have no depth and their noses will not stick out: a problem which increases with the distance between actor and audience and therefore not so vital in a tiny hall. A bigger problem with horizontal lighting in any size of auditorium is that the shadows will be life size. As the angle of light increases, the shadows will decrease until the point where the light is coming vertically from above the actor and the shadow is all contained within the area of the actor's feet and is therefore barely noticeable. But such a vertical light, if the only source, plays havoc with the face: eyes become black sockets and the highlighted nose assumes Cyrano de Bergerac proportions. Few actors use the nose as a principal means of dramatic expression, and their main acting features, eyes and mouth, are in darkness. The compromise angle, between vertical and horizontal, to produce visible sculptured actors, with a shadow of proportions that they can dominate, is somewhere within the range of 30°–60°.

We have therefore positioned our light with a view to attempting fulfilment of two of the basic requirements for stage lighting: to make the action visible and to make it as sculptural as possible. And we have our priorities right by putting visibility first and foremost: there is no point in actors acting if the audience cannot see them. With only one source we are hardly in a position to use light to control atmosphere, although if the play were generally cheerful I would probably put in a bit of pale rose, and if it were sad I should go for the palest steel tint.

Light is an important way of selecting the audience's vision and concentrating their attention upon the dramatically significant area of the stage. With but one spot, selection is limited to differentiation between stage and auditorium. This may seem obvious but I have known small theatres with quite large lighting rigs where this was not achieved and light spilled all over the proscenium arch, the audience and even the auditorium walls. Our single spot must therefore be focused carefully so that the light is contained within the stage picture: if at all possible, the spot should have a barndoor to shape the beam because if we select a position of the focus knob to give sufficient width, we shall almost certainly have too much height; and the height of the light should be no higher than to catch the head of an actor standing at the back of the acting area.

If I had two spots only, I would place them in the auditorium ceiling but would use positions towards the side of the auditorium rather than in the centre. If the width between the side walls was not a great deal more than the proscenium opening, I would put the lights on the side walls, but if the auditorium was very wide, I would try to choose ceiling positions just a little further apart than the proscenium opening.

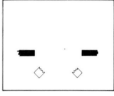

C

All our light is still coming from the front and the scene will therefore be rather flat but, because the actors are receiving light from both sides, they will be a little bit more sculpted than when we had one spot only. We can increase this dimensional effect by putting slightly different tints in the spots: perhaps gold in one spot and pale gold in the other – or possibly rose in one and gold in the other. Or, if it is a cold situation, perhaps steel in one and steel tint in the other. Alternative possibilities are gold and open white (i.e. no colour) or steel and open white. It is all a matter of experiment: indeed, playing with a couple of spots and a bundle of gels is the best way to find out about controlling the colour of the stage picture.

With spot number three, it is time to go backstage and perhaps time to introduce a key into the lighting: I like light to have motivation. This motivation need not be a logical source such as moon, sun or a practical light fitting, because it all depends on the style of the particular show. It could be a spot shining through a window or it could be just a spot providing a cross or backlight. Experiment – but remember the remarks about light in our discussion of spotlight number one.

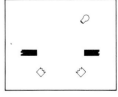

D

Back to the checklist! This lamp is really going to start doing something for *sculptural modelling*, and by changing colours during the show (think of access when you position the lamp) we can start getting *atmosphere* under control. If we are building up a rig by buying equipment, it is now time to acquire our first profile spot which will give us more accurate control of the beam, and we can always get interesting effects such as leaf dapples by cutting shapes in foil and inserting in the gate slot (*not* in the colour frame runners!)

Another way of dealing with three spots is to have only one in the auditorium, and use the other two focused across the stage from positions immediately behind the proscenium. On the whole, I prefer the two out front, but stage lighting is full of discoveries based on trial and error – and it is only when you have such a small amount of equipment that you have time available for experiment.

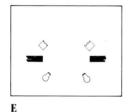

E

If I had four spots only, in the interests of balance I would probably place two foh spots in the auditorium and the other pair immediately behind the proscenium to light across the stage. Keep them highish, because apart from considerations of sculpting the actors and keeping their shadows short, if the spots are too low one actor will tend to cut off light from another. (Only very sensitive actors can use light to upstage their fellows: insensitive actors cannot even find the light!)

By the time we are using four spots, I would favour having all foh as profiles. This has rightly become standard practice because it enables us to contain the light within the proscenium arch and to trim the edges quite accurately by means of the shutters. Moreover, profile spots have less spill outside the main beam and, after all, it is the actors that we wish to light, not the audience. Certainly I have suggested earlier that the first two spots should be fresnels, but in a desperate situation (and you cannot get more desperate than lighting a play with one or two spots!) the fresnel has more width to its beam and is much easier to adjust.

With these four spots we have just the beginnings of selectivity: not the selection of clear cut areas but we could concentrate attention on one side of the stage or the other – if we had dimmers. When do we start introducing dimmers into the scheme of things? If it is a question of buying, not yet. Renting? Probably not yet. Borrowing? Yes, provided it is not a case of dimmers versus extra spots. I think that spending money on dimming is relatively unwise until you have about six spots. Unless, perhaps, you are producing nineteenth century romantic opera.

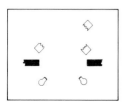

F

Have spot number five instead and use it for a keylight.

Number six could go centre, immediately behind the

proscenium. With two crossing spots, you are almost certain to have a dark hole in the middle: so focus the new spot straight up the centre of the stage. Perhaps not dead centre for fixing or focus: that will depend on the shape of the set. With some dimmers you could now get increased control of selection of the area of stage that you would like the audience to look at. And as for visibility – well, the number of dark holes should be decreasing.

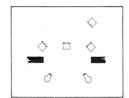

G

Spot seven is a real breakthrough. Four spots behind the proscenium and we can really start talking about Number One Spot Bar without blushing! If we number the spots A, B, C and D, an actor standing on the OP (actor's right) side of the stage would be lit by spots A and C, while an actor standing on PS (actor's left) would be lit by B and D. These spots will not do much for an actor standing immediately underneath them, but this position will be lit from the foh. When we have only a few spots, the duty of the spot bar is to provide visibility upstage.

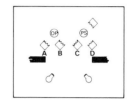

H

And yes, you are quite right, the on-stage lighting is now getting out of balance with the foh, so spot number eight should go out into the auditorium. Place it centre where it can fill the gap between the two side foh, which for architectural reasons have probably had to be positioned too far to the sides. And spot number nine could be foh also, so that we can carry on with our aim of lighting the actor from both sides to give as much sculpting as possible. If we label these four foh as W, X, Y and Z, actors who were lit by A and C upstage will be lit by W and Y when they come downstage. If this were a programmed learning machine, the next question would be 'what lights an actor stepping downstage from B and D?'

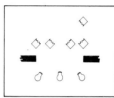

J

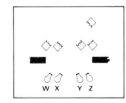

K

But this is not a definitive factual recipe for lighting: it is just one lighting designer's thoughts and anyone who has reached spot number ten by practical experiment will be so full of ideas that they will have dozens of possible uses for it. I think it is quite likely that it will find use as another key light: perhaps one from each side of the stage, or perhaps two keys from the same side with a difference of colour or directional quality. With our ten spots, we have quite an adaptable rig. If the stage is required to vary atmospherically in terms of warm and cool tones, we could split our lamps into pinks and blues, or we could have mainly pinks with just a few blues, or perhaps some neutrals. There are a lot of possibilities and much of the detail will be a personal response. But not too personal: the light must be relevant to the production style.

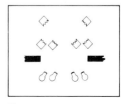

L

8
The lighting design process

Whatever the scale of operation, lighting, like any other design process, is based upon a sequence of logical management decisions which provide a framework for creative imagination to flourish. Creativity grows out of a designer's subconscious, planted there in the long term by the experience of looking at life through their own and other peoples eyes and, more immediately, by immersion in the details of the particular production currently under design. It is inevitable that many creative decisions will be illogical (that's what makes them creative!) but they have to be taken in a logical sequence.

THE LIGHTING DESIGNER

Someone has to be in charge of the lighting process and is normally called the lighting designer. This lighting designer is not some rather grand person who appears towards the end of the rehearsals and implies: 'Right! You, Director, have done your production bit and you, Designer, have done your scenic bit. Stand aside and I will light the result of your (pathetic) efforts!' The lighting designer is part of the production *team*, indeed an important contributing member of that team: but the director must have the ultimate decision. The only way to get shows off the ground is to appoint directors, give them dictatorship powers, and fire them if things do not work out. Good directors do not flaunt their dictatorship powers: they need to be hypersensitive to human feelings because they have to be able to draw creativity out of people. But the lighting designer must be prepared to give the director whatever the director wants, even if the lighting designer can hardly bear to look at the result. In practice, a lighting designer is likely to say 'Right, I'll certainly do it that way, but don't you feel that it will . . . ?' If the reasoning is convincingly argued, it will probably carry the day – but good lighting designers, like good directors, have to be students of human nature.

The lighting designer may, of course, be the director. Or the scene designer. Or the stage manager. And is very often the chief electrician. But there is a lot to gained from having a separate person for the job. Apart from the director and scene designer having quite enough problems without getting involved in the nitty-gritty details of lighting, there is often a conflict of interest between light for the actor and light for the scene. The inevitable compromise is probably best arrived at by a third person.

Stage management is difficult to combine with lighting because stage management is essentially a back-stage task, whereas lighting requires a view from the front. There is much to be gained from the chief electrician doubling as lighting designer: they must obviously work very, very closely, but it is helpful if one person can concentrate on deciding what ought to happen, while another concentrates on making it happen. Moreover, unless the production company own the theatre, the electrician's responsibility will be primarily towards the theatre, while the lighting designer is concerned with the requirements of the production.

But, whatever the distribution of duties in a particular situation, someone must be in charge. Let us call that person a lighting designer and follow the design process through their eyes.

Text Study

Almost by definition, the play script or music score is the starting point. Before any initial discussions with the other members of the production team, the lighting designer should read the script at least twice, first for overall 'feel' and then for detail, concentrating on the dialogue rather than any stage directions which the director may ignore – especially those in an 'acting edition'. For a work with music, the score will be listened to until absorbed. This text study will stimulate ideas but the lighting designer will try to keep a very open mind at this point.

Discussion

Just how early the lighting designer should be involved in the production planning process will depend on the type of show. For a straightforward comedy or whodunit, there is little need for lighting involvement in complex decisions about precisely where the sofa should be in relation to the window, or indeed the colour of the sofa cushions. But it is essential that the lighting designer see the scene design before construction starts. In professional theatre, the final scenic design is almost always a scale model and this should be more common in amateur theatre. It is much easier for everyone, especially director and actors, to 'read' a model than sketches. The lighting designer may be able to suggest simple modifications which will simplify a lighting problem. On a model such a modification can be made quickly, easily, and cheaply, with a penknife; on finished scenery it requires tools, time and money.

If the production is in any style other than a naturalistic interior, the lighting should be considered much earlier. The director and designer will no doubt have a series of discussions at which ideas will gradually develop: the lighting designer should be present for parts of some of these discussions. Apart from ensuring that light is considered as an integral part of the production rather than something to be grafted on later, the lighting designer is usually welcome as an occasional third opinion on the progress of the production's concept. It need hardly be pointed out that there is no welcome at these discussions for the type of lighting person who has a one-track mind about lighting problems and a negative attitude to solutions. Buckets of cold water are out of place in production planning, and should be applied very occasionally and as a last resort. Constructive creative thinking must be the order of the day.

Most production problems in theatres arise from communication difficulties of one kind or another. In lighting design they arise from the necessity of using words to describe visual situations. Visual communication between the director and the design team is helped enormously when scene designers draw story boards showing the sequence of how the various scenic elements are used and giving some indication, however impressionistic, of their vision of the lighting.

Style Decisions

Arising from these discussions, there should be broad agreement as to style before either rehearsals or scenic construction start. During rehearsals, ideas may change and will certainly develop – so the production team must remain flexible and communicative. There should be consensus between director, choreographer and design team as to how the script will be staged and the contribution to be made by lighting. Light will normally be expected to provide supportive illumination and sculptural modelling for the actors and their environment. But will it be softly diffused or have stabbing beams? Will light select acting areas? And/or will it establish shifts in atmosphere? Will there be any special effects? Will the colours be subtle tints? Or more strongly romantic hues? Or more saturated contrasts? Or a clear penetrating white? How naturalistic?

Rehearsals

The wise lighting designer pops into rehearsal from time to time. A series of short random visits will gradually build up a feeling for the whole production as the script is transformed into a detailed realisation which, hopefully, bears some resemblance to the earlier discussions. The sight of the lighting designer should inspire confidence in the director and actors. As the production takes shape, and ideas of acting, scenery and wardrobe gradually become reality, lighting designers are the one unknown creative factor, their ideas remaining a sheaf of papers. Will the lighting designer pull the rabbit out of the hat? 'Surprise us', the actors' eyes seem to say. To appear at rehearsals and chat over a cup or glass is a wise psychological move: the actors may later understand black spots and, more important, move out of them.

Befriend stage managers. They can provide vital information from the prompt book. Directors often become so involved in the production that they believe they have passed on information to other members of the team. Remarks to an actor like 'that is where you switch-on the table lamp' or 'as you break left, a blue light will fade up on you from the front' may be news to the lighting designer.

Plans

Design involves paperwork where the key lighting design information is recorded on the lighting plan and the cue synopsis.

The lighting plan is made from the scenic groundplan and, like that plan, is normally to the scale of 25:1. Many theatre plans are still to the old scale of $1/2$ in to 1 ft, but for practical lighting purposes this is acceptably close to the metric 25:1. The lighting plan is drawn on a sheet of tracing paper pinned over the scenic plan. After the lighting equipment has been drawn, enough scenery is traced through to relate the geography of the set to the lights.

A lighting plan has two functions: *working out* and *communication*. It is the sheet of paper on which lighting designers actually work out how they will light the show: the instruments to be used, their positioning, how they will be coloured, which

Instrument symbols on plans
Any symbols can be used provided that a key is drawn on the plan. But communication is easier if symbols conform, either to the international standard:

Flood   Fresnel

Profile   Focus

Effect

or to scale stencils where a particular manufacturer's models are specified:

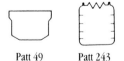

Patt 49   Patt 243

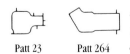

Patt 23   Patt 264

dimmers will feed them, and where they will be focused. All these decisions are best made by sitting down at a blank plan with pencil, eraser and a flagon of strong coffee. Always choose the thickest available tracing paper, capable of withstanding alterations from the lighting designer's most important tool – the eraser. Having worked out the grand design, copies of the plan are used to communicate the designer's intentions. Apart from informing the rest of the lighting team, copies should go to stage management, scene designer, production manager, etc, so that they too have some idea of the lighting crew's intentions. One hopes, often in vain, that they will consider the plan before making the changes of mind to which theatre people are addicted. But even if they do not actually look at the plan, it is a good psychological principle to shower copies around. Plans drawn on tracing paper can be reproduced easily by the dyeline process, while those for studios or small halls may be small enough to reproduce on photocopiers.

The aim in plan drawing is to produce a document which is so explicit that if the lighting designer mailed it to an electrician, then that electrician could get every instrument hung, coloured, and connected, without meeting or telephoning the designer. Normally the focus information would not be printed on the plan, except perhaps some rough notes like UL (up left) or DR (down right) to enable rigging electricians to point the instruments in approximately the right directions.

Any type of symbol may be used to indicate the various instruments provided a key is drawn in the margin to indicate what each symbol means. There are internationally agreed symbols for profile, flood, fresnel etc, but these only indicate basic instrument family types. Symbols used on lighting plans normally need to relate more specifically to particular manufacturer's models. It is helpful if the symbol is to scale, because if there is space for the symbol on the drawing, then there should be space for the instrument on the stage. There is no absolute standard for noting colour and control channel numbers: I put the colour number inside the symbol and the dimmer number outside. Horizontal bars are easy to indicate within the two dimension of a plan. Vertical booms are not so easy – usually the base is marked and a dotted line run off to a drawing at the side of the plan.

A major problem in the process of lighting design is that decisions have to be made and plans drawn before all the necessary information is available. Ideally, the plan would be drawn after the final run-through in the rehearsal room, but many equipment decisions normally have to be made before that time. Lighting designers and their plans must be flexible. New ideas will keep coming after the plan has been drawn, but it is much better to have a plan to alter than to have no plan at all.

DESIGN DECISIONS AT THE DRAWING BOARD

The sequence of decisions to be made at the drawing board is summarised below. Some of the basis on which these decisions are made has already emerged in earlier chapters and more detailed discussion is included in later chapters.

Identifying Areas

If the production requires the stage to be divided by areas for independent selection, these have to be determined. These areas are rarely symmetrical in size, shape, or distribution – and are at actor face level which does not correspond to the area of lit floor.

Identifying Colours

If the lighting style is to include colour mixing, the stage is divided by colours, establishing which areas in drama need both warm and cool toning. Perhaps some can be neutral? In a musical there may be areas where more saturated 'reds', 'blues' and possibly 'ambers' are required in addition to face 'neutrals'.

Deciding Specials

There are two main categories of 'special' instruments. Some will be required to highlight specific scenic features, and some to light actors in situations where the size and shape of the beam is so critical that none of the generally focused area lights will suffice.

Establishing Priorities

Priorities need to be established for the allocation of resources. There is rarely enough equipment or time to meet all the requirements of our ideals. How vital is that two minute special effect? Enough to justify removal of several lights and dimmers from two hours of general use?

Choosing Instrument Positions

Instrument positions are chosen to give the best available angles for lighting the chosen areas in the chosen colour ranges. Specials and effects are similarly positioned.

Choosing Instruments

Instruments are allocated, starting with the ideal type for each position, then reallocating to make the best use of equipment actually available.

Selecting Filters

Filters are selected by converting general 'warm', 'cool', 'reddish', 'bluish', 'hot', 'fruity', etc, colours into specific filter numbers.

THE CUE SYNOPSIS

The expression *lighting cue* is used to denote a change in the lighting. The *cue* is the starting point of the change and the *cue time* is the duration of the change. A *cue state* is the lighting arrived at after completion of a lighting cue. Thus *cue five* represents lighting moving to a new stationary *cue five state*. These would normally be written as *Q5* and *Q5 state*.

The cue synopsis is a list of Q numbers and timings with a note of where they occur in the script, how long they last, and roughly what happens. This 'what happens' is not a detailed prediction of which particular instruments will be used, but a description of the cue in verbal terms such as 'build blues downstage right' or 'fade out everything except sky and Lear on top step'. The cue synopsis should be prepared at a point in the rehearsals when the form of the production has stabilised. If possible it should be prepared prior to the penultimate run-through in the rehearsal room so that it can be checked against the action during the final rehearsals. No matter how pressing are the demands on everyone's time at this point it is fatal to start the final countdown of 'getting in', lighting and dress rehearsing, unless there exists a cue synopsis to supplement the lighting plan.

The synopsis is prepared by a committee which, like all committees, has a precise optimum number of members. One essential person missing and its decisions will be taken on insufficient evidence, one inessential person present and its

LIGHTING CUE SYNOPSIS

ACT TWO   'WAIT UNTIL NIGHT'

PAGE	ACTION	Q	TIME	LIGHTING
41	OPENING OF SCENE	O.L.	PRESET	MOONLIGHT THRU' WINDOW HALL BACKING ON FIRELIGHT
41	FRED & MARY ENTER	1	SNAP	STANDARD LAMP ON SOFA AREA [SOFT/ROMANTIC]
43	ANTICIPATE FRED'S RISE	2	25s	CHEAT UP FRONT CENTRE + DRINKS TABLE
45	MRS G'S ENTRANCE	3	SNAP	WALL BRACKETS ON ALL AREAS TO ABOUT ¾
47	DOOR BELL	4	30s	BUILD NEARLY FULL FOR COMEDY BUSINESS
50	BRIAN'S EXIT	5	20s	CHEAT DOWN EDGES
57	END OF SCENE	6	3s	FADE TO BLACKOUT

decisions will take twice as long. The cue synopsis committee consists of director, choreographer (if appropriate) designer and stage manager with the lighting designer in the chair. The minutes of the committee consist of the cue synopsis and this should be widely circulated as soon as possible. This synopsis has columns for Q-number, Q-timing, script page number, stage action, and lighting. As each cue is decided, the position is marked in the stage management prompt copy. If the duration of a cue is uncertain, the dialogue is spoken (or music hummed) at the correct speed until the point in the script by which the light change should be completed: a watch will give the elapsed time in seconds.

It is amazing how the discipline of constructing such a synopsis can force the production team into realising problems and making decisions – not just in lighting matters but in all departments. However the production team often say they are too busy to meet. If so, the lighting designer should prepare a synopsis for circulation. (The stage manager who is going to 'call the cues' will almost certainly be happy to join the lighting designer in preparing this draft synopsis.) People who hesitate to commit themselves on a blank sheet usually love to edit, and directors are no exception. So the list will come back with alterations and annotations which can be averaged out and recirculated. But it is easier for all the team to sit down and discuss it together in the first place!

Communicate Intentions

Intentions are communicated to electrics crew, production manager, stage manager, scene designer and director by circulating copies of the lighting plan and cue synopsis. It is advisable to point out to them anything vital that they might otherwise overlook.

Check Intentions

During the final run-throughs in the rehearsal room, the lighting designer makes a final check of all the intentions of the plan and cue synopsis by comparing the action during each cue state with the planned areas, colours, specials, etc.

9
Implementing the lighting design

Design phase over, planning complete. In our mind's eye we can see the 'lighting look' that we want for the show. We hope that we have devised a rig using the right lights in the right places. Will it all work? We cannot be sure until the equipment is rigged and focused so that we can begin to paint the stage with light by balancing the contributions from the various sources. Creative ideas and splendid technology will achieve little unless they integrate with each other and with all the other elements in the production mix. Theatre is about communication with an audience during the real time of a performance. It is about what *is*, not what might have been. Ideas must become reality and this requires organisation.

In staging a show, every department needs organisation, but the lighting department needs more than most because lighting people can only really do their thing when everyone else has finished doing theirs. Time is the enemy and time creeps up fastest and most devastatingly on the electrics. Consider the situation. The actors have a lot of rehearsals and if one or two of these (actors or rehearsals) are total disasters, all is not lost: there is time for a rethink. Scenery can be redesigned, its models made, modified and discarded. It should be obvious in the workshop whether a crinoline lady can get through a door. If the production team hates the paint colour, there is still time to experiment with alternatives. Costumes can be fitted in time to be altered. Props can be chosen and changed.

All these activities can be carried out away from the stage: they belong to the rehearsal room and the workshop. But what about lighting? It cannot be rehearsed until it is created, and it cannot be created until every instrument is physically in position, supplied with electricity, and focused. And it cannot be focused with any degree of facility until the scenery is complete and in position.

The potential of lighting in the creation of controlled performance space is virtually limitless. But full exploitation can only really come from experiment. Experiment which requires time: and that time, for the reasons discussed, is not normally available. It is, therefore, essential that the lighting process is highly organised so that available lighting time can be used creatively. We have discussed the sequence of events in the lighting design process. Let us now consider the organisation required to enable an effective realisation of the lighting design.

SCHEDULES

Planning of the entire production process, and especially the lighting, has to proceed from a basis of time available. Time and money are interrelated, but in the theatre there are occasions where money just cannot buy time. At the risk of being boring, it must be emphasised continually that theatre is about communication and one idea that gets carried through and projected to the audience is worth a dozen ideas that remain stillborn in the designer's mind.

Theatre people achieve miracles against the clock: they work to time scales which might be considered rash in other sectors of industry. But, whereas it might be justifiable to aim to condense three hours work into two, it is certainly improvident to plan for four or more hours to be squeezed into two. Therefore, before embarking on detailed planning, it is necessary to agree a draft schedule for the allocation of stage time.

PREPARING EQUIPMENT

What is the factor most likely to wreck our careful planning? In my experience and observation, a major source of frustration in lighting is *poorly maintained equipment*. There are quite enough problems without having to cope with equipment which is dirty, mechanically doubtful (jamming and wobbling) and electrically intermittent. And lack of mechanical and electrical maintenance is not just frustrating, it is dangerous.

Owned equipment is the easiest to maintain because ownership normally allows controlling access to it. If regularly used by sympathetic hands, lights are virtually everlasting provided they are checked over regularly. However, rough handling can devastate the mechanics and unfortunately it takes quite a lot of experience to discover just the right amount of pressure necessary to make the required focusing adjustments. Whether equipment is left hanging or kept in store will depend on frequency of usage. Either way it is essential that a continuous maintenance programme be undertaken, with a special check carried out prior to each production so that defects may be remedied.

Rented equipment from whatever source should be clean and safe. The best hired equipment is electrically, optically and mechanically as new – the only indication of long service being the quality of the paint finish. Some hire equipment has been known to fall short of this standard: you tend to get what you pay for, although the mushrooming of small hire companies in recent years has made lighting hire into quite a competitive business. Always report any problems to the rental company boss and insist on immediate replacement of any faulty equipment.

Installed equipment on a rented stage can be the most difficult maintenance situation. It may be in the hands of a resident staff beyond our control, and the maintenance will therefore be as good as the staff. On many stages the equipment is excellently maintained. If not? Alas, the realistic, if depressing, solution may be to build into our planning the contingency assumption that some lights may not be as bright as they should be, and that it may just not be possible to get full benefit from shutter and lens movements. A supply of thin strong flexible wire is a useful standby for counteracting the sagging tendency of spots with slipping tilt-locks.

The following check lists indicate the required degree of preparedness:

Optical Check

- Reflectors clean?
- Lenses clean?
- Lens properly positioned with retaining clips, springs, etc.?
- Lamp not nearing the end of its life?
- Lamp properly seated in holder?

Mechanical Check

- Lens tube or focus knob moving freely?
- Shutters moving freely yet remaining where positioned?
- Hanging bolt complete with wing nut? (or spigot, if on a stand?)
- Safety chain for each light?

Electrical Check

- Each instrument fitted with correct plug?
- Plug correctly attached?
- Cable tail in good condition?
- All cables with correct plugs and sockets?
- All cables visually inspected for breaks or cracks in outer sheath?
- Is the cable sheath grip taking the strain in all plugs and sockets?
- Are all control channels working?
- Any blown fuses to mend?
- Spare fuses standing by?

Accessories Check

- Enough barndoors available (with doors that will stay where put)?
- Enough irises, masks, gobos?
- All colour filters cut to size, labelled, numbered and framed?
- Enough clamps and boom arms?

RIGGING

If planning is good and equipment well prepared, all that is required for smooth rigging is co-ordination between the lighting and scenic departments. It is usually better if the lights over the stage are hung before the scenery goes up – probably while it is still coming in the door. Then, when the scenic chaos starts, the lighting crew can move to the side of the stage or into the auditorium to rig foh. Whatever happens, it must happen as a result of inter-departmental rational discussion. A free-for-all on stage will soon lose all the potential time saving from pre-planning. The rigging process will demonstrate the quality of our planning, and, if this planning is good, we might get all the instruments positioned, coloured, and plugged to their correct dimmers without the use of a screwdriver. Or that should certainly be our ideal.

The easiest bars to rig are those on a suspension system which allows them to be lowered to a working height of three or four feet above the stage floor. The procedure is:

(1) Hang all instruments loosely on the bar by their hook clamps.

(2) Slide them along the bar until the spacing is correct.

(3) Tighten all hook clamps.

(4) Fix all safety chains.

(5) Plug up each instrument, ensuring enough slack cable to focus freely.

(6) If the bar is not internally wired, run feed cables along it, securing with plastic tape.

(7) Pull out all shutters on profile spots.

(8) Fit any gobos into profile spots.

(9) Fit all barn doors.

(10) Fit all colours.

(11) Point each instrument in its approximate direction (unless there are two which share a dimmer but cannot be reached from one ladder position: in this case, focusing will be easier if one is initially tilted to the horizontal).

(12) 'Flash out' to ensure that each instrument is lighting. If the cables are to be plugged in after the bar has been flown, write the socket numbers on each plug top.

(**Above left**) a simple **Rigger's Control** allows channels to be faded up or down for checking and focusing without requiring an operator in the control room.

(**Above right**) more complex **rigger's controls** allow most facilities of the control desk, including channels and memories, to be accessed from a simple hand-held keypad usable anywhere in the theatre.

Then, and only then, should the bar be hoisted away to operational height.

Bars on fixed suspensions are not much fun to rig – as anyone who has tried to fit a barndoor from the top of a ladder will testify. So it helps a lot to ensure that matters like fitting barndoors and pulling shutters have been attended to before taking a spotlight up a ladder. And the same applies when fixing instruments to vertical booms.

Safety

Safety in rigging cannot be over-emphasised – both electrical and mechanical safety. Time is always short and since 'the show must go on' there is always a risk of cutting corners. And when people are tired, both mentally and physically, there is always the possibility of omitting to tighten one of the many nuts, or overlooking a cable which is not properly anchored to the bar with tape to take the strain off the plug and socket connection. The only way is to check, check and check again.

FOCUSING

With all instruments hanging and lighting, it is time to start focusing. Under ideal conditions, the scenery will be complete and dressed with all furniture and properties. And all will be quiet to allow the lighting staff to concentrate. But under normal conditions, at best there will be noise and chaos as the finishing touches are put to the scenery; at worst this will be so behind schedule that our concentration and voices will have to compete with the sound of power tools. On the few occasions when I have had ideal focusing conditions, the piano tuner has arrived. But the probability of noise and chaos during focusing is yet another reason for good advance planning.

The process of focusing needs a minimum of three people and a fourth is desirable. It is just possible to be a one-man-focusing-band but, to push-up the dimmer knobs and climb the ladders as well as stand in the light beams is asking too much from even the most versatile lighting designer. Sometimes it has to be done. But it takes time that is rarely, if ever, available. The three people in the team are the lighting designer, the electrician up the ladder, and the board operator. The desirable fourth is someone to hold the ladder steady. All members of this team do not need to be equally experienced. Obviously, the more that the electrician up the ladder knows about the equipment, the better: but it is surprising just how quickly an inexperienced person can focus if given good clear intelligent instructions like *up, down, left, right, bigger, smaller,* etc. At this point anybody should be able to work the board, since all that is required is to bring the channels on one by one when their number is called. If the machine is not labelled well enough for this simple purpose, there are likely to be problems when the complex stages of plotting and operating are reached.

Throughout the focusing process, it is essential that the lighting designer remains on stage, moving about in the light from the instrument being focused to check that it will light the actor, watching where the end of the beam hits the scenery, and giving instructions to his team in a clear, cheerful, and encouraging voice. To ensure that we know exactly what light is coming from a particular source, it is better to have only one spot alight at a time unless we are checking an overlapping join with another spot. Incidentally, it is surprising how much time can be saved if, as a matter of routine, the next instrument is switched on before the previous one is switched off. It also ensures that the stage never goes to complete blackout: this is not just more pleasant for working, it is safer!

In small studio theatres, the board can often be moved from the control room to the stage for focusing. And for larger stages, 'rigger's controls' offer small hand-held units allowing individual channels to be raised or dimmed from the stage without anyone being in the control room.

Our focusing should aim to be accurate, clean, efficient and safe. The essence of *accurate* and *clean* focusing is:

- Ensuring that the actor is lit everywhere in the area which has been allocated to that particular instrument.
- Overlapping smoothly the light beams of adjoining areas.
- Trying to make the beam edges of actor light hit scenery in an unobtrusive way.
- Normally using a soft edge which will be unobtrusive on both actor's face and scenery.
- Remembering that, since they make such positive visual statements, there has to be a logic for any hard edges.

Focusing is more likely to proceed smoothly and efficiently when we:

- Don't light the instrument until we are absolutely sure where it goes (it gets hot quickly!).
- Do adopt a clear code for talking to the board operator. When we shout a number we mean that dimmer up followed

by everything else out – unless we add the words 'as well'.

- Do talk in terms of the actual adjustments that are available on the particular instrument which is being focused.
- Speak loudly and clearly, keeping the ends of sentences up.

And a *focusing safety* check . . .

- Do make sure that the ladder is stable – and has somebody holding it.
- Don't leave tools at the top of the ladder.
- Do make sure that all adjustments are left tight.
- Don't place any strain on cables when adjusting instrument positions.
- Do make sure that no instrument is left in a position where it will foul on anything – such as a curtain track.
- Do fade in each new light before dimming out the old, so that the stage never goes totally black . . . and it saves time.

LIGHTING REHEARSALS

Focusing over, comes the great moment of truth for the lighting designer. Will all individually focused lights add up to the pictures that have until now existed only in the imaginations of the production team? And have all members of that team really been imagining the same thing? I have never conquered the flutter of heart beat and the sinking of stomach that accompanies the moment of taking the plan from the stage to the auditorium and calling for a blackout prior to composing the opening cue state.

   This is the moment when the lighting team move around. On the board we must now have the finest, most experienced, operator available to us: plotting a show is much more difficult than operating it – indeed if the plotting is good, most reasonably intelligent and sensitive people can be taught to operate relatively quickly. On stage we need the member of the stage management team who knows the detailed movements of the actors and who is going to control the performance. On either side of the lighting designer sit the director and scene designer. The lighting designer has the plan and cue synopsis. The stage manager has cue positions marked up in the master prompt copy and the lighting operator has a special copy of the cue synopsis with the time *between* cues indicated on it. On non-memory controls, operational problems depend on the time available between cues for resetting, rather than the doing of the cues themselves.

Thus prepared, we are off! The lighting designer calls for the channel numbers one after another, balancing intensity levels as he goes, until there is a provisional cue state to offer the team. The director moves the stage manager around the stage to check the light level around the door and by the sofa. The designer comments on the colour of the sky. A few adjustments, and the board operator is instructed to 'Plot It!'. The operator must be allowed all the time needed to write down or electronically record a precise plot: there is no point in carefully balancing stage pictures if we may never see them again. As the lighting rehearsal proceeds, it tends to accelerate as the team becomes familiar with the range of lighting possibilities available – or, as one cynical director put it: 'Once we have found out what we have not got'. Cynics have also pointed out that many shows have fewer cues in the second half: a combination of tiredness, and time running out at lighting rehearsal.

There are occasions, particularly for short runs of performances, when it may be desirable that lighting designer and board operator be the same person. This has only become possible with recent advances in technology because it is essential that, when the jobs are combined, the lighting designer can take the control desk into the middle of the auditorium for the lighting rehearsal. This is a moment when the production team must really work as a team: and teamwork is difficult if the team leader is stuck in a box at the back of the auditorium or on a perch at the side of the stage. Having the desk in the middle of the stalls is not always practical for the middle price-range of control systems but it is relatively straightforward for the most expensive and for the cheapest. It is possible to place the smaller desks exactly where required: on stage for focusing, in mid-auditorium for rehearsal, in a control room (perhaps in a studio theatre, improvised with screens) for performance, and locked up in a cupboard at night. With the larger boards it is possible to have a special associated stalls unit.

With good memory boards and experienced operators it is often possible to leave the finer details of balancing until technical and dress rehearsals with the actors. Providing the general shape of the lighting has been plotted, adjustments of a point upwards and downwards are often simpler to make when all the actors are present – and with a memory, the right balance can be achieved and instantly recorded without disturbing the flow of an actor rehearsal.

Simplified Plans

The 1:25 plan is established as an excellent method of working out a lighting rig and communicating it to the electrics crew. However, the size of the plan does rather limit the mobility of the lighting designer, and the format does not immediately indicate which lamps light a particular area. For the lighting rehearsal and subsequent technical and dress rehearsals, it is often more convenient for the lighting designer to condense the essential information on to a standard 8×5 index card. The only numbers on the card are channel numbers and these are written within arrowed symbols indicating direction. These symbols can be drawn in coloured inks to give an approximate indication of, say, warm and cool or pink, amber and blue. 'Specials' can be listed in a corner. The plan for a small show can often be condensed on to one side of a card, leaving the reverse for an abbreviated cue synopsis. A big show may require one side for stage and the reverse for foh. A jumbo musical may need separate cards for coloured (atmosphere) channels and neutral (face) channels. But three cards is the maximum that should ever be necessary to condense the complete plan and cue synopsis. Such cards are normally only meaningful to the designers who prepare them, but they are solely for their use and enable them to watch the show from all angles. On previews and first nights they can even be slipped into a programme – together with an extra card for making notes! See page 151 for an illustration of a simplified plan.

Magic Sheets

Computer technology allows the possibility of direct access to the dimmer control system. A light pen on a video screen is one possible method. But recent developments include using a mouse as a 'light brush' on areas of a stage plan to bring control of that area's lights directly under the lighting designer's painting hand.

Board Plots

The tricky part of board operation is plotting: not so much the actual writing down, but the decisions as to how a particular cue is to be done. These plotting decisions vary with the type of board. On directly operated resistance slider dimmers will the next cue need knees, elbows or a length of wood? On a two pre-set board shall it be a new preset or just nimble fingers? With a multi-preset multi-group system the choice could be new preset or new group, or perhaps a combination of these plus nimble fingers. Everyone develops their own solution as they become familiar with their particular system.

When operating, I always try to plot to a simple but fixed routine so that, in a panic, *cockpit drill* will take over. The information to be recorded on a plot divides into two categories: *preparations* and *actions*. The time available between cues for resetting is often the critical factor: it is certainly the most blood-pressure raising factor on opening night, although, by a couple of performances later, one always wonders what all the panic was about. However, I certainly have always found it advisable at the point of 'electrics go' to be able to react to an action instruction written beside the cue number where my marker (a clothes peg) is resting. And then, having completed the cue, my need is to go to a clear instruction on what to prepare next.

ACT TWO — SWITCHBOARD PLOT (MINI 2 – 18 WAY) — 'WAIT UNTIL NIGHT'

Q	TIME	TYPE	ACTION	LEVELS			AFTER Q
OPENING LIGHT ✗	PRESET	—	R ↑	$\frac{13}{8}$ $\frac{14}{9}$ $\frac{15}{4}$ $\frac{16}{6}$			
1 ✗	SNAP	BUILD	G ↑ (R ↓)	$\frac{3}{5}$ $\frac{5}{4}$ $\frac{8}{7}$ $\frac{11}{6}$ $\frac{13}{8}$ $\frac{14}{9}$ $\frac{15}{4}$ $\frac{16}{6}$ $\frac{17}{7}$			R → Q3
2	25s	BUILD	BY HAND ON G	$\frac{3}{4}$ $\frac{4}{4}$ $\frac{10}{3+}$			
3	SNAP	BUILD	R ↑ (G ↓)	$\frac{1}{5}$ $\frac{2-4}{7}$ $\frac{5}{4}$ $\frac{6}{6}$ $\frac{7-12}{7}$ $\frac{13}{8}$ $\frac{14}{9}$ $\frac{15}{4}$ $\frac{16}{6}$ $\frac{17}{7}$ $\frac{18}{8}$			G → Q5
4	30s	BUILD	BY HAND ON R	$\frac{1-6}{8}$ $\frac{7-12}{9}$			
5	20s	CHECK	(G ↑) R ↓	$\frac{2-5}{6}$ $\frac{8-10}{6}$ $\frac{11}{5}$ $\frac{13}{8}$ $\frac{14}{9}$ $\frac{15}{4}$ $\frac{16}{6}$ $\frac{17}{7}$ $\frac{18}{8}$			R → ACT THREE
6	3s	FBO	G ↓				G → ACT THREE

Everyone has their own personal format for a plot sheet. All sorts of things like finger prints, coffee stains, etc rapidly become landmarks as one drives through a performance. A board plot cannot show absolutely everything. There is a human element in timing which is what live theatre is all about. But with a clear plot, the operator can relax at the moment of

'Go' into giving full attention to the timing. The typical plot (for a two-preset) shown here is not offered as the only format, but it does indicate the sort of information that has to be recorded.

On memory boards the levels are not normally written down on the plot since they are electronically filed for instant recall. But, apart from this, the plot needs to list the same categories of information. Indeed the potential of memory boards for totally fluid lighting means that there can be a considerable increase in the number and complexity of sequential and simultaneous cues.

TECHNICAL REHEARSALS

The first rehearsal at which lights are used with the actors is the technical rehearsal whose purpose is to integrate the actors with their stage environment. At a 'tech' the actors concentrate on such matters as manoeuvring around furniture, coping with doors, timing entrances, etc. rather than the finer nuances of characterisation. The actors and the technical cues have to be coordinated carefully: the actors (and their director) should not expect the technicians to get everything right first time – this is the technicians' first rehearsal whereas the actors have been at it for weeks. Some tricky sequences will need to be repeated – and when 'going back' sufficient time must be allowed for any adjustments to plots to be written carefully and the board to be properly re-set. When technically rehearsing some shows, it is possible to jump from 'cue to cue' – that is to pass over sections where there are no cues. However, it is essential to remember that operational problems are not associated so much with doing cues as preparing for them. When cues occur in fast sequence, the sequence needs to be rehearsed without any stops so that the operator is working within the reality of the time that will be available in the performance.

At this rehearsal, it will almost certainly be necessary to rebalance dimmer levels in some of the cue states. How much of this can be done during the rehearsal will depend on the modifications required, the complexity of the show and the type of control board. Unless there is a memory board, notes should be made and the rebalancing left until after the rehearsal. Notes should also be made of any adjustments required to the focusing of the lights.

Technical rehearsals are always tiring and frequently depressing. The key to success lies in avoiding panic.

DRESS REHEARSALS

Whereas technical rehearsals are very much stopping occasions, the aim at dress rehearsals is to keep going – stopping only if the continuity really falls apart. Unless the number of cues is very small, it is unwise for the lighting designer to make changes during the running of a dress rehearsal. Much better to make notes during the rehearsal, then arrange priorities and take action afterwards. Dress rehearsals, especially the final one, should always be organised as performances with the stage manager in charge. The lighting designer should only intervene in cases of extreme chaos. When the rehearsal grinds to a halt, it should always be the stage manager who ascertains whether all departments, including the lighting operators, are ready to start again, and tells them which cue state they should be in.

It is just not practical to work a lighting control while reading a script. All amateur companies should follow the professional practice of working on cue from the stage manager (or whichever member of the stage management is controlling the performance). Traditional red (warn) and green (go) cue-lights are virtually obsolete because they can be missed so easily. When cueing by voice, the method is important. With 'Go electrics Cue 25 please', it is difficult to know exactly on which word the cue is supposed to start. 'Electrics Cue 25 (pause) GO' is positive and provides a second stand-by on which to tension the hand muscles.

PERFORMANCES

If all planning and rehearsals have gone well, the actual performance should be smooth and fun. Let's hope that the first night is not an anti-climax!

But something is sure to go wrong. When a lamp blows, or a cue is late, keep calm. Remember that we have all been living with the details of the show and its lighting for a long time, probably weeks. The audience have just come in: they do not know what is supposed to happen. If we carry on smoothly without jerks, they may never realise that we have been overtaken by what, to us, is total disaster.

Graph Plots

If the production is having more than a very small number of performances, or if it is likely to be revived at a later date, the lighting plan should be corrected. What happened is not always what was planned! The cue synopsis should be expanded into a graph plot containing the information in the specimen plot illustrated. The graph plot in conjunction with the plan forms a complete record of the production's lighting.

ACT TWO — *GRAPH LIGHTING PLOT* — 'WAIT UNTIL NIGHT'

LOCATION			FOH						SPOT BAR						WINDOW		BACKINGS	FIRE	PRACTICALS	
CHANNEL			1	2	3	4	5	6	7	8	9	10	11	12	13	14	15	16	17	18
LANTERNS			23	23	2x23	2x23	23	23	123	2x123	123	123	2x123	123	223	2x60	2x137	123	STANDARD LAMP	WALL BRACK
COLOUR			54	17	54	54	17	54	54	47	17	47	54	54	50 change 21	17 change 14	3	5/6	—	—
SETTING																				
Q	TIME	PAGE																		
OL	PRESET	42													8	9	4	6		
1	SNAP	42			5		4		7			6			8	9	4	6	7	
2	25s	43			6	4	4		7		3+	6			8	9	4	6	7	
3	SNAP	45	5	7	7	7	4	6	7	7	7	7	7	7	8	9	4	6	7	8
4	30s	47	8	8	8	8	8	8	9	9	9	9	9	9	8	9	4	6	7	8
5	20s	50	0	6	6	6	6	0	0	6	6	6	5	0	8	9	4	6	7	8
6	3s	57	0	0	0	0	0	0	0	0	0	0	0	0	0	0	0	0	0	0

THE GET OUT

After the final performance, the lighting should be restored to an appropriate 'square one' condition. This is discussed in a later chapter, but any check list is likely to include:

- Dismantle any temporary rigging.
- Restore any equipment which has been moved back to its usual position.
- Return all rented and borrowed equipment promptly, including all accessories. (Rental companies and lenders are only human: customers known to look after equipment get better service and keener discounts.)
- Store other equipment carefully: shutters pushed in, gobos removed, barndoors folded, cable tails coiled around suspension arms. Any defective equipment labelled with details of repair required.
- Re-usable colour filters filed away by size and number.

10
Lighting plays

The process of designing lighting for a play starts, as it does for any type of performance, by establishing the contribution expected from light. The lighting style that will be appropriate for a particular production of a particular drama text is not at all easy to determine. However, most styles stem from some degree of realism, even if that realistic connection is rather distant. Most plays are about people. Their behaviour, to be credible, needs to relate to the behaviour of ourselves and the people around us. And we the audience will probably relate more readily to the play if its environment has some connection, however tenuous, with the world that we live in. Consequently, many production styles come under a heading that might be called *heightened realism*. Acting and scenery become an exaggerated and/or simplified version of the reality of 'normal' life. Therefore, in seeking the lighting style for a play, a useful starting think-point is reality. To what extent, and in what ways, will the light depart from an attempt to copy the natural lighting sources in the sky and the artificial light sources developed by mankind's determination to overcome the daily cycle of darkness?

Total naturalism – or, at least, as close as we can get to it on the stage – is the style with the clearest logic and therefore the easiest to understand, if not always the easiest to achieve. Therefore, to illustrate the type of thought processes that go into designing a drama rig, let us work through an imaginary show. Let us take that theatrical cliché, the box-set play with french windows and a drinks table behind the sofa. This may be one of the duller lighting situations, but it is also one of the most difficult: it can be much easier to organise a dramatic sequence of individual stabbing beams than to get a smooth drawing-room full-up which illumines yet pays more than just lip-service to all the other lighting aims which we have set as our ideal.

Set Design

The play is set in an out-of-town drawing room (see ground plan overleaf). Across the upstage corner is a french window

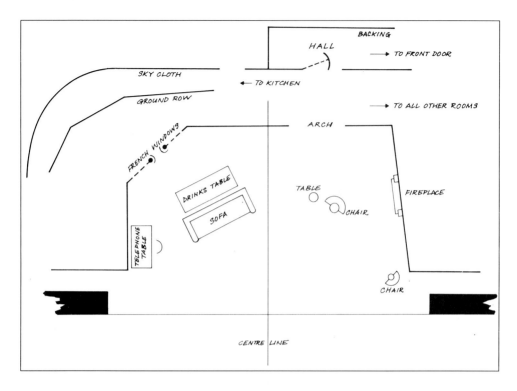

Scenery ground plan opening on to a fragment of garden with hedge and a distant vista of church spire against sky. As this distant vista is only about four feet away at most, we shall have to rely on actors not reaching heavenwards and spoiling the illusion. Upstage is an arch leading to a small hall with doors to all parts of the house: perhaps we should not probe too deeply into the details of its architecture. On the stage left wall is a fireplace. Furnishings are simple. Actors making an entrance through the all-purpose arch and moving downstage have a simple choice of a sofa to the right or an armchair to the left. Behind the sofa is a drinks table and beside the armchair a small table provides somewhere for an actor to rest her glass. Down right is a desk to support the telephone and down left is a chair that nobody sits in. It faces upstage to focus attention inwards: if anybody does sit there, it is only because the author has forgotten, not only to write any dialogue, but to provide an exit line.

Style

For this play, *naturalism* or *realism* are the key words. This realism might perhaps more properly be called stage realism, because life in a box set has conventions which are only loosely based on behaviour in a real world. Nevertheless, for lighting purposes, real and natural are the key words. Light in this production will try to behave like natural light in real life.

Light Sources

In our daily life, there are two types of light source: natural and artificial. When we act out the drama of life in a room at home, light may come from the sun or moon through a window. Or it may come from electric light fittings. If the sunlight enters the room by only one window, it still illuminates all the room by reflection from surfaces such as walls, floor, furniture, etc. Thus, if we stand near the window, that side of our face will be highlighted. The other side of the face will also be lit, but to a lower intensity by reflected light. Similarly, at night, a wall bracket light fitting will light all the room by reflection but with certain directional highlights.

When we remove one wall of the room to let an audience watch the drama, we could still rely on reflected light if the audience were no larger than perhaps three rows deep. But as soon as the audience increases in size, we have to project the stage action. In lighting terms, this means that we can no longer rely on natural reflection of light from single sources such as a jumbo sun lamp outside the window by day, and electric lamps on the walls by night. We must introduce all the paraphernalia of stage lighting to reinforce these natural light sources.

This may all sound very obvious, but it is important to go through this kind of thought process when working in *any* lighting style. Having found a style, we must establish *key* lights which will make positive lighting statements – often a positive directional statement, or a positive colour statement, or both. In addition to the key, there will be a lot of unobtrusive light sources whose function is to project the idea of the key by cheating in balanced light from non-key directions or with non-key colours. In the naturalistic style of play under consideration, the keys would be sun, moon, and practical lamps.

Outside the Window

In box set plays, views through windows are very important in establishing such details as whether the house is in town or country, whether the room is ground floor or upstairs, the time of day, the weather, etc. In nature, there is one big celestial light source, the sun by day and the moon by night. Light from this source illuminates everything that we see through the window

— buildings, roof tops, trees, sky, etc. Light entering the room through the window may be direct light from sun or moon, but it is more likely to be light reflected from the various outside surfaces such as roof tops, hedges, etc.

In a theatre, having one single source does not work. Apart from differences in reflective quality between scenic and real surfaces, we need a *controlled* light. And to control the light we need one set of lighting gear to deal with what is seen outside, and another to deal with the light coming through the window.

The main problem in lighting scenery outside a window is to make it retreat. Such scenery is usually within a very few feet and often close enough for an actor to touch the church spire. A portion of sky is usually included and this means hanging floods to give a smooth light at the top. The number of colours required will depend on the number of meteorological conditions demanded by the script and the director. The minimum is likely to be a couple of blues: a deep and a not so deep, with the actual filters depending on the strength and toning of the blue paint on the cloth and the range of blue skies required in the production. The pair of filters should be rather contrasty because a really deep blue filter helps to put beef into a blue sky, even when the predominant effect is from, say, the pale steel of the other circuit. If a dirty and gloomy or perhaps lavender sky is required additionally, then it may be necessary to have a third colour: but think twice before doing so because it may use up equipment, circuits, and space that can be ill afforded.

In any case, such requirements are often better dealt with from an electrics groundrow at the bottom of the sky. It is difficult to get an illusion of depth into a skycloth without having light at the bottom as well as at the top. This means that, between window and cloth, there has to be a scenic groundrow to mask the electrics groundrow. This scenic groundrow helps the illusion of depth because it provides a middle distance for the audience eye to focus on and relate near (window) and far (sky) distances to. Light from a groundrow usually has to be in a minimum of three colours: a couple of blues (they should be slightly different from the filters in the top floods) and some sort of sunrise/sunset colour in accordance with the demands of the script. Check on the height of the scenic groundrow. I once specified an electrics groundrow to sit on the stage floor, only to find that the scenic pieces were seven feet high: I had to scrounge a couple of floods on stands to do the job. Any scenic pieces standing in this area, or features painted on the cloth, will be lit by spill from the sky floods and bounce from the back of the window, but if there is a prominent architectural feature – like a church spire – and we can spare a small spotlight, then a highlight can enliven the whole picture.

So much for what we see through the window. What about the light coming through? As a general rule, it is better that there should be as few instruments as possible: we must avoid multiple shadows from an excess of sources. In our plan, there are many possible positions for these spots. They could hang on a bar between window and sky, but the light would come from so high an angle that it would only register on the tops of the window glazing bars, on the floor, and on actors only when very close to the window. They could be on a boom upstage, but then the light would only register on the upstage glazing bars and the downstage walls of the set; again, an actor would have to be very near the window or desk to be hit by the light. If the light hits though the window from a downstage boom, it registers on the parts of the window bars that the audience can see, it can make a pretty pattern on the upstage wall of the set; and it not only lights actors in quite a large area of the set, but lights the aspect of them which is visible to the audience.

Fresnels, with their soft wide-angled light are often the favourite instruments here. The average ten foot high window lights well with two pairs in each of two colours. Of a pair, one instrument lights the top and the other lights the bottom with very little overlap so that we get only one window-image projected. With one pair in pale yellow, and the other in pale blue, we have a range of mixing possibilities. Both colours for cool morning light, yellow alone for afternoon and warming as it dims towards sunset, blue only for the moon.

Theatrical effect often has to take precedence over strict accuracy as to behaviour of sun and moon in relation to the compass. Remember that sunlight/moonlight is often funnelled through other buildings, so the vertical direction can be most telling – like the low angle of a setting sun across the bottom section of a window, or the rising sun striking only the roof tops from a low angle as it comes over the horizon.

But read the script carefully and discuss with the director: no point in providing a feat of meteorological and astronomical detail if the window curtains are going to be closed!

Backings

The lighting of a backing outside a door requires the same approach: a light on the backing itself, and a separate light through the door. A spotlight set to shine through an open door ensures that, on exit, an actor walks off into light and, on entrance, is backlit. Be careful with the angle though: an entrance can be spoilt if we see a shadow of the actor getting ready to enter. Entrances and exits are very important moments for the actors and the play: they are usually the time when audience concentration on a particular actor is highest. If the intensity of light on the backing is high, the actor will be in silhouette and facial expression will disappear. Backings must therefore be balanced very carefully with on-stage actor light. Soft selective spotlighting is best: a flood should be used only when a spot is not available. Small backing spots can often be hung from brackets screwed to the backs of scenery flats.

Acting Areas

Having designed the peripheral areas, we come to the part of the stage where the action is. The first step in planning is to break the stage down into separately controllable areas. This can be done in an arbitrary way by devising a grid of equally sized units, perhaps nine areas based on downstage, midstage and upstage – subdivided into left, centre and right. Such a system covers all eventualities in an approximate way, but it should only be resorted to when we do not know the precise areas required by the production.

In the play under consideration, there may be only one area: the whole stage. If it is a farce with a plot depending on mislaid trousers, there may be no need to break the stage into areas. Or

Production areas

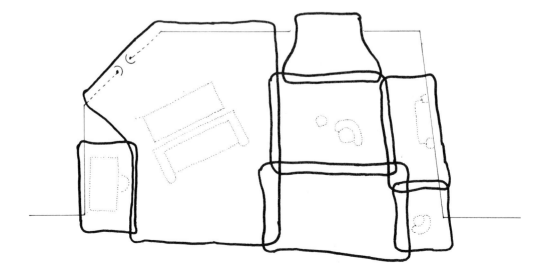

there may be just two areas: a small one based on a table lamp by the telephone, and a big one which is the rest of the stage. Or an intimate scene on the sofa may provide a third.

Consider the possible sequence of the play that may inhabit our set. Act One – early evening starting with quite a lot of daylight, but progressing to the point where the practical light fittings must be switched on. Act Two – midnight with dying firelight and a touch of the moon, enter couple who switch on standard lamp at the sofa followed by Apologetic Discoverer who switches on a blaze of artificial light. Act Three – morning after the night before, a bash of sunshine.

Already this simple scene synopsis has told us a great deal about separately controlled lighting areas. Watching rehearsals and talking with the director will reveal more. For example, after switching on the standard lamps and having a preliminary skirmish on the sofa, one character may decide to fix drinks: it is likely that the drinks table area will have to be cheated brighter. (Incidentally the first cue was a conscious snap switching cue, the second will be a slow subconscious cheat.) That setting sun in Act One will have to be fiddled with care so that the appropriate action area is left a little brighter than the rest – that is, becomes another controlled area.

An analysis of areas will probably produce a list far longer than can be dealt with in practical terms. So the list has to be refined. Close examination usually reveals that what we thought to be two separate areas are so nearly identical that they can be regarded as one.

In seeking to establish areas, beware the director who says: 'Well there is the sofa, and the chair, coming through the door, and looking out the window . . . and, of course, the drinks table.' Such a director is often thinking back to the old style of lighting where the stage was covered with a wash of light from flooding equipment and spotlights were used to highlight chairs, etc. The actors moved from one highlighted puddle to another, passing through a flat murky wash in between. Modern lighting techniques join the spotlights together to form a balanced controlled directional light throughout the acting area.

Thinking in Section

The process of identifying the ideal production areas and, if necessary, reducing them to a practical number, will result in outlines on the plan that look rather like a series of spotlights focused on the floor. We must not fall into the trap of thinking

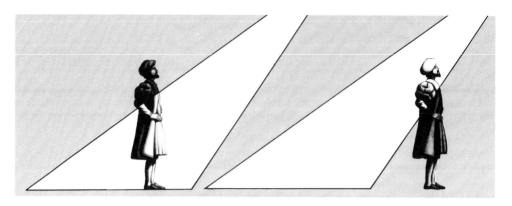

Actors may stand within a pool of light on the stage floor yet their faces will miss the light. And stand outside that pool of light with faces fully lit.

that the actors will be lit if we focus spotlights in this way. Since the light will need to strike the actor at an angle in order to reach eyes and teeth, the light at actor's face level will not correspond with the lit area of floor. Thus actors may stand within a pool of light on the floor, yet their faces will miss the light. Or, indeed, an actor may stand outside that pool with face fully lit. So when we mark out an area on our plan we are thinking of that area at face level – and in consequence the light will spill on to a larger surface of floor and walls than is apparent from our marked area on the plan.

Another problem of thinking and working in plan is the difficulty of imagining the angle at which the light strikes the actor. As a general rule, the light will hit the actor at a much more vertical angle than looks likely from the plan. With experience, lighting designers develop an instinct which enables them to look at plans and visualise the angle. But this intuition only comes after involvement in many productions where the designer has checked sections and plans against the reality of the production. These sections need not be beautiful drawings of the entire stage: quick thumbnail sketches will tell quite a story provided we draw the horizontal and vertical measurements to the same scale.

In (A) the actor is standing under the spot and we have already discussed the advantages (good sculptural modelling) and disadvantages (poor visibility due to eye and mouth shading) of such a vertical light. In (B), he has moved upstage and we are gaining visibility at the expense of modelling. In (C) he has moved so far upstage that the light, though providing good visibility, has become very flat. In (D) the light cannot possibly reach the actor's head because a border is in the way. In all cases, we can note the height of the actor shadow on the back wall of the set.

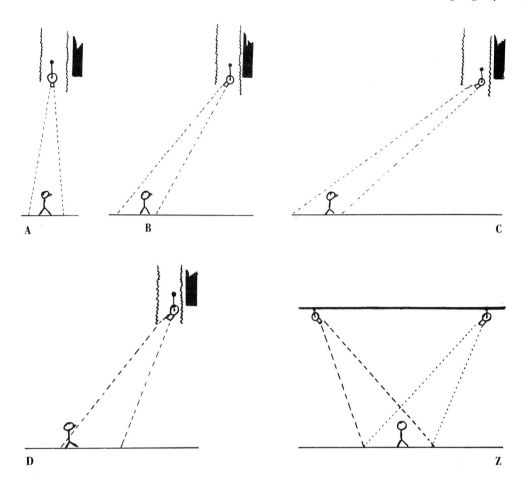

This type of section, drawn up and downstage, is the most generally useful. However, if we want to consider the effect of side lighting angles on the actor standing directly underneath a spot bar, we can draw a section across the stage as in (Z). No section, however, will tell us the whole story because the light will rarely be hitting the actor directly from the front or from the side. It is more likely to be a pair of lights forward of the actor but displaced to the sides. And as they are moved sideways (along, say, a spot bar) the angle at which they hit the actor will decrease. This is not easy to work out on paper and, to be honest, I use a large amount of guesswork. Fortunately my guesses have improved with practice!

With luck, the lighting designer will be able to walk about the actual stage on which the play will be performed. Even if the lights are not hanging, it is possible to look at the positions and gain some idea of the angle that they will provide. Stand in the actor positions and point at a light; your arm will show the angle at which the beam will hit the actor. Use your other arm to extend the line of the beam behind you (you will look as if you are playing at aeroplanes!) – this will show how far the lit area will extend behind the actor. Go back to the drawing board both before and after the show. Relate the plans and sections to the actuality of the light on stage; relate it to the feel of the light as you personally stand on stage, and relate it to the way it looks on the actor when you watch from the auditorium. This relation of cause and effect, of paper and reality, is the only real way to learn about lighting.

Fan Setting

In a naturalistic play, the light coverage has to be smooth and even with the possibility of being not only divided into areas, but also given a directional emphasis which is logical in terms of light sources. The simplest way to achieve this is by setting the instruments in the form of a fan.

We have seen that the most economic way of getting a light which both illuminates and models is to use a pair of spotlights from the front and to the sides of the actor, one to each side of the face. Thus, three areas will require six spotlights. In the illustration, an actor standing in area A is lit by spots 1 and 4, in area B by 2 and 5, and in area C by 3 and 6. Spots 1, 2 and 3 are set to cover the stage in a fan from one side and spots 4, 5 and 6 to make a fan from the other side. The spots overlap slightly so that the actor moving across the stage goes smoothly from one area to the next. Smoothness is also helped by the throw distances and angles remaining reasonably constant across the stage: as a result, very little balancing of individual dimmers is required to maintain an even light.

Fan setting

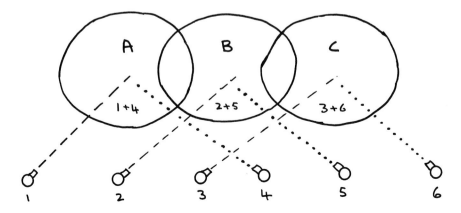

To introduce a directional emphasis, spots 1, 2 and 3 could be set to a slightly higher intensity than 4, 5 and 6 – or *vice versa* to give an emphasis from the other side.

In our play, a spot bar hanging immediately upstage of the proscenium will produce a useful fan of light starting at a line approximately five or six feet upstage of that spot bar, assuming that the spot bar is about fifteen feet above the stage. The higher the bar then the further upstage will be the start of a useful fan. In a play of this kind the normal setting is not very deep and basic area coverage can be achieved with two fans, the upstage from spot bar and the downstage from foh. Because of the architecture, foh spots often have to be fixed where we can have them rather than where we want them. The angle is nearly always too frontal and is often also too low. The quality of the foh light will therefore be different from the spot bar light and it is important to have a considerable overlap between them in order to avoid an abrupt change in light quality as the actor moves between upstage and downstage.

Offstage Side of the Face

Actors are easy to light in the middle of the stage. The problems are at the sides of the stage and stem from the difficulty of getting a light beam to hit that side of the actor's face which is nearest to the wings. In an open setting, light can be directed from offstage, but light beams cannot pass through the walls of a box set. In a daylight scene it is natural that the side of an actor nearest to a wall would be less bright; but if an actor in a night scene is standing near a wall bracket, then naturalism requires that the wall-side of his face should be the brightest. In a box set, we can only deal with the problem by focusing the extreme ends of the spot bar to their own sides. This is the natural position for the first lamp in a fan setting, but it is a tricky operation because of the necessity of trying to avoid excessive flare on to the adjacent scenery wall. Such a flare of spill light will take the audience eyes upwards and away from the very actor upon whom we are trying to focus attention. Similar problems arise with the foh, because side foh can usually only light the opposite half of the stage – or, if we are lucky, the opposite two-thirds.

Perches

Spots fixed to the proscenium walls on each side of the stage or to booms as far downstage as possible, are called *perches*. The

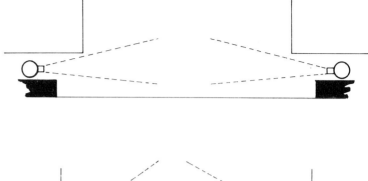

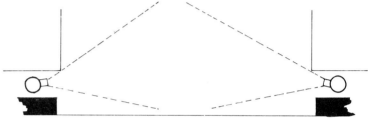

Perch angles: (Top)
Proscenium wider than set; **(Centre)** Proscenium same width as set; **(Bottom)** Proscenium narrower than set.

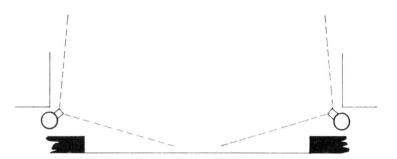

name comes from platforms, still fixed to the proscenium of some older theatres, where electricians once perched to trim the carbon arcs which were a basic light source from this position in bygone times. These perch positions can provide a useful light for the offstage side of the face in the downstage area, as well as providing general modelling cross-light. Their degree of usefulness depends on the extent to which they can light upstage, and this in turn depends on how the scenery fits within the proscenium arch (see illustration above).

Practicals

A naturalistic set is normally dressed with all the furnishings and props to be found in a real room. This includes electric light fittings which, when they actually light, are known as *practicals*. If they have diffuse lamps and opaque shades, it is easier to avoid their causing a distracting flare. As practicals are part of the decorative scheme, they should be selected by the scene designer rather than by the lighting designer. If a practical is to look like a plausible light source, the edges of the spotlights hitting adjacent walls must be carefully trimmed. For example, a spot should not actually hit a wall-bracket fitting but should fuzz out just below, so that the practical appears to be casting a glow downwards and outwards. Careful balancing helps plausibility and practicals should be on individual dimmers wherever possible. If a practical cannot be on a dimmer, or has to share a dimmer, a selection of lamps of various wattages should be available at the lighting rehearsal.

Colour

We have been discussing the play only in terms of selecting controllable areas, and the direction from which we should light those areas to get a good compromise between visibility and dimensional modelling. What about *colour*? We need to apply a similar approach to that used for discovering controllable areas. The belt and braces solution is to cover every area twice, having what amounts to two lighting rigs – one in warm tones and the other in cool tones.

Apart from the economics of such an approach, the script and production may not require such lavish provision. So it is back to production analysis. Colour in a naturalistic play tends to be used to denote morning, afternoon, sunlight, electric light, gaslight, candlelight, etc. If it has a happy/sad meaning, it is often because a clever author or director has twisted time and season to match the emotional situation. Which areas require a colour variation? Do we need a different colour for artificial light or will the natural warming of slightly dimmed lamps do the trick? Or will cosy ambience come from a more localised light rather than from colour? Very often a colour toning of the stage can be achieved by a few spots set in open focus to colour wash the stage. Whatever way we plan to use colour, the decision must come from the style and demands of the production.

Footlights

How about footlights? These are very rarely installed in new theatres. At one time a major light source, they were rejected with the development of modern techniques because of the distorted effect produced by a strong upward light on the face. They were further rejected on architectural grounds when neuroses started to develop about the proscenium arch acting as a barrier between actor and audience. Have they any value? It certainly can help an actor's face to have a little soft upward light to counteract some of the heavy shadowing that can result from an overabundance of top light. The problem is that, when we use enough footlight to gain a significant result on the actor's face, we also introduce shadows of a particularly irritating nature. This effect is called 'rising shadow' because it is higher than the actor and the shadow height varies as the actors move up and downstage. Furthermore there is likely to be not one shadow but a whole series corresponding to the individual lamps in the footlight.

Nevertheless, in a box set comedy, if a footlight is available, I like to try a little – but carefully balanced to the point just before rising shadow becomes noticeable. Apart from the slight lift to the lighting, there is a psychological lift to the actors. A warm glow can help actor confidence, and, contrary to most theorists, many actors *like* to have a barrier between them and the audience. A famous comedy actress, who certainly developed an immediate rapport with each and every audience, once said to me, 'Can I have footlights – I need them for protection against the devouring monsters out there!'

Choosing Instruments

Our discussions on lighting the play have so far been concerned with decisions about angles of light and positioning of the instruments to achieve these angles, rather than with type of instrument to be used. I believe this to be a fundamentally correct approach. I first put crosses on my plan to indicate the positions of the lights. Then I add basic indications of direction (using such shorthand as little arrows with reminders like DR and UC for down right or up centre) and colour type (such as W, C or N for warm, cold, neutral). Only when I feel certain about the positions of the lights do I decide which types of instrument I would ideally like to use in each of these positions. First as a family (i.e. flood, fresnel, profile, beamlight, etc) then as a particular instrument with the appropriate beam angle to cover the required area on the throw distance from the decided position. Finally I rationalise – possibly deciding to use PC or fresnels spots in some positions because they will be faster to focus than profiles and schedule time looks distinctly short. But more probably because I have to use equipment which exists rather than the equipment I would ideally like to have. Lastly I convert my notions of colour tones into actual filter numbers.

A Typical Plan

Piecing this discussion together into a typical lighting rig for our box set, what do we get? (See pp 130–1.)

Outside the window, circuits 21 and 22 cover the sky in a darkish blue and a paler blue. At the bottom 25 and 26 cover in slightly different blue tints, and a third groundrow circuit gives a warm sunset. In the middle of the flood bar, a profile spot (23) highlights the church spire on the groundrow. The boom has a couple of warm fresnels (27) and cool fresnels (28) for the window. Outside the doors, 19 and 20 deal with backings and entrances/exits.

On the spot bar, 1, 3 and 5 form an upstage fan from stage left and this corresponds with the fan of 8, 10 and 12 from the right. 4 and 9 light across the downstage area to counteract the flattening effect of the foh. 2 and 11 give a controlled flood of cool light across the stage. Number 6 punches up the light on anyone delivering an entrance or exit line at the door, and 7 lifts the light on anyone who may be otherwise over-silhouetted while standing in front of the window.

From the perches, 13 and 14 provide a fanning cross-light to centre and upstage right, while 16 and 17 do the same from the other side. The lower perches, 15 and 18, provide a soft fill to their own sides of the stage.

In the tradition of the permanent basic rigs of many theatres, fresnels have been used on the No 1 spot bar, with profiles from the foh.

From the front centre 31, 32, 33 and 37,38,39 provide a fan coverage, while 35 provides a fill. 34 and 36 are a cool wash. From the sides of the auditorium, 39 and 41 give cross-lighting to centre, while 30 and 40 carry this cross-light on to their respective far sides.

This is not, repeat not, *the* ideal way to deal with a box set play, it is merely *a* possible way of approaching the problem.

Using More Instruments

Lighting positions in box sets are often limited by a ceiling. Obviously when there is a ceiling, it is not possible to hang spot bars in positions other than the downstage area immediately behind the proscenium. A backlighting spot bar becomes

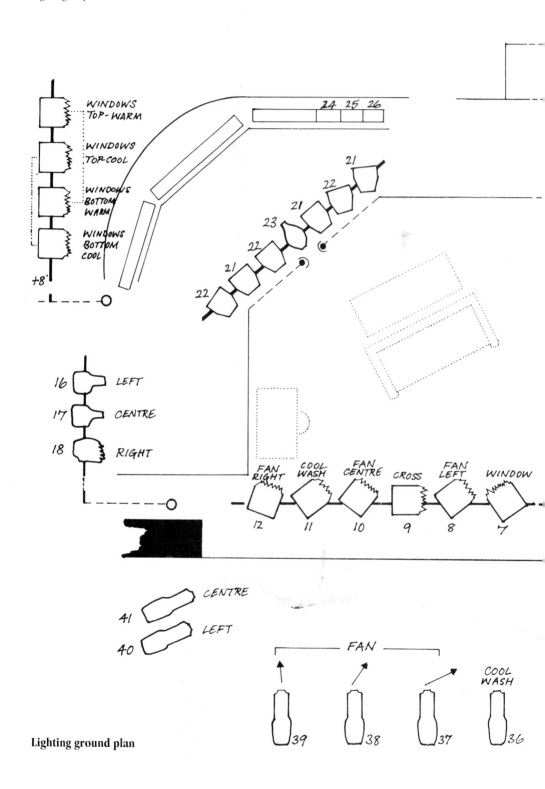

Lighting ground plan

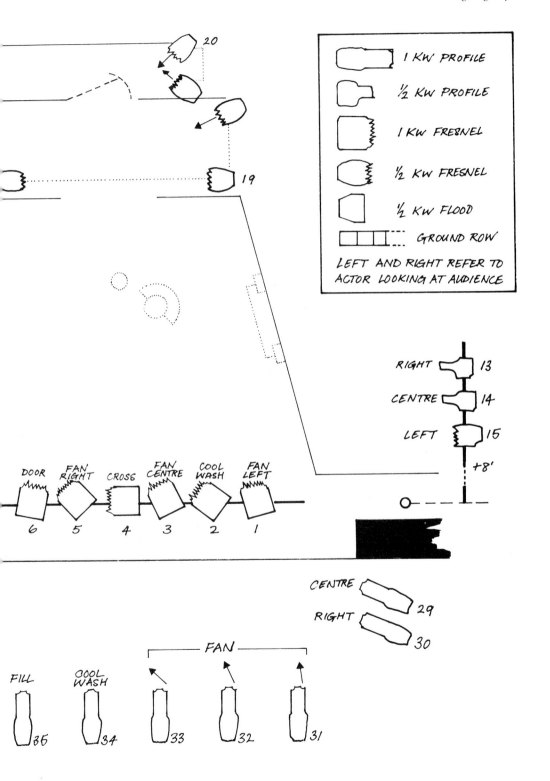

20

1 KW PROFILE

½ KW PROFILE

1 KW FRESNEL

½ KW FRESNEL

½ KW FLOOD

GROUND ROW

LEFT AND RIGHT REFER TO
ACTOR LOOKING AT AUDIENCE

19

RIGHT 13

CENTRE 14

LEFT 15

+8'

| DOOR | FAN RIGHT | CROSS | FAN CENTRE | COOL WASH | FAN LEFT |
| 6 | 5 | 4 | 3 | 2 | 1 |

CENTRE 29

RIGHT 30

FAN

FILL   COOL WASH

35   34   33   32   31

possible when there is no ceiling, and a midstage spot bar can introduce a more dimensional modelling angle of light into the upstage areas. If more lights are required in the downstage position, the first spot bar can be double banked – an additional bar hung next to, and slightly higher than, the first one.

Using Less Instruments

We may, for reasons of economy in instruments, electricity or time (all of which equate to some extent with money) be forced to use less lights. They would probably be discarded from the plan in something like the following order: 35, 4 and 9, 34 and 36, 23, 7. Then the perches would become one open-focused spot per side, backings would reduce to one lamp per circuit, the side foh would shrink to one per side. The boom would become three fresnels, then two fresnels. Flood bar and groundrow would become whatever old floods or bits of batten were available, and the boom would reduce to one spot on a stand. Before long, we would be down to the fundamental situation of our *first steps* as discussed in Chapter 7.

Balancing

Once all the lights have been hung and focused, the procedure for arriving at the various cue states runs parallel to the thought processes at the drawing board. The starting point is the key source. First the view outside the window is built up, followed by the light coming through the window. Then the spot bar and perches which light from the same direction as the window (i.e. key source) are added. Instruments from the other side are now balanced to a slightly lower intensity level so that the light appears logical in terms of the window.

For an artificial light source, the same sort of procedure is applied. First the practical light fitting, then the spots which light the appropriate area from a logical direction and, finally, addition of other angles, with careful balancing to ensure that the scene remains logical in terms of the practical light fitting.

FLASHPOINT: AN EXAMPLE OF A BOX SET PLAY

It would be very difficult indeed to design a set more box-like than *Flashpoint*. The box was a nissen hut army barrack-room with side walls running up and downstage, and back wall running across and parallel to the front of the stage. The door was upstage centre with a window on each side, and the furnish-

ings were limited to beds and lockers positioned with appropriate military respect for symmetry.

Flashpoint was a naturalistic play and the lighting had to relate logically to its apparent source: two naked bulbs hanging from the (supposed) ceiling. Their harshness provided the clue to filter choice for the lighting instruments – none. Apart from a touch of gold tint in the backlight and a touch of blue in a couple of front-of-house circuits, this was an open white play.

In planning the light outside the windows, some licence was taken in the interests of dramatic effect. The entire action of the play took place at night, but night in an army camp is neither black nor blue – logically there would be some warm light from street lamps, other huts, etc. However, at the climax of the play when one soldier is holding his fellows as hostages at gunpoint, 'arc-lights' were directed onto the hut and subsequently shot out. The impact of such a scene is helped by maximum contrast and so the external light on the window was restricted to a deepish blue.

The Mayfair, unlike most London West End theatres, had a reasonable stock of lighting instruments and so it was possible to light the play entirely from the theatre's own resources. The Mayfair's foh positions are good, with a bar over the front stalls seating giving a particularly sympathetic face angle (being a tiny theatre – 310 seats – ladder access to this bar is not a problem).

Flashpoint at the Mayfair Theatre

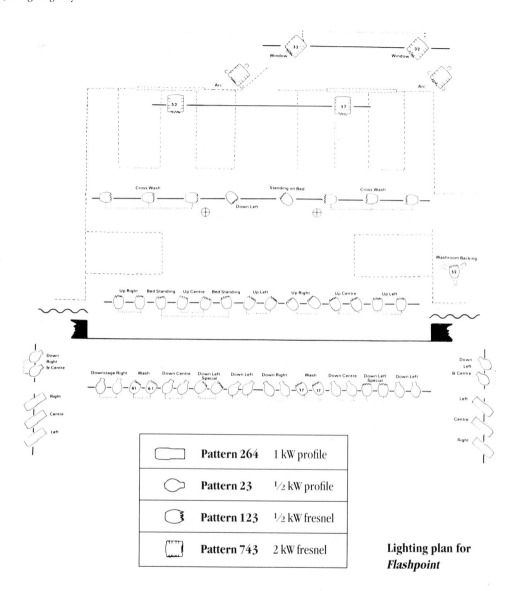

	Pattern 264	1 kW profile
	Pattern 23	½ kW profile
	Pattern 123	½ kW fresnel
	Pattern 743	2 kW fresnel

Lighting plan for
Flashpoint

As can be seen from the plan, six pairs of spots on the first stage bar were focused in a conventional fan-setting on the up-stage areas (left, centre, and right); and, similarly, six pairs from the foh bar cover the downstage areas. All areas had a comfortable degree of overlap.

The midstage bar gave a cross-wash and the auditorium side-bars (again set in a left/centre/right configuration) helped to model the actors from the lower angle. The only instruments that could be called specials were some fresnels focused to highlight a couple of key scenes in the play – one played standing on the upstage right bed and the other in the down left corner. (Throughout, the terms right and left are used to indicate the actor's left and right, not the audience's.)

There were two upstage bars. The bar just downstage of the back wall of the set gave a simple wash of backlight on the actors, while the last one backlit the windows. The 'arc-lights' were 2 kW fresnels – on stands to give the appropriate horizontal angle for dramatic effect when the window was broken and the room lights switched off.

The cues worked on two levels: naturalistic switching off and on of the practical room lights, and subtle changes of emphasis where the lighting balance was cheated so that the audience's concentration was controlled in a subconscious rather than conscious way. The plot worked easily on a two-preset control system.

"FLASHPOINT" —— CUE SYNOPSIS

Q1	5 secs.	BUILD WINDOWS (BLUE)
Q2	SNAP	ROOM SWITCH ON
Q3	SNAP	WASHROOM ON
Q4	CHEAT	CONCENTRATE USL
Q5	CHEAT	RESTORE
Q6	CHEAT	BUILD STANDING ON BED U.R.
Q7	CHEAT	REBALANCE FOR SITTING ON FLOOR
Q8	5 secs	FADE TO BLACKOUT

—— INTERVAL ——

Q9	5 secs	FADE UP AS WAS
Q10	CHEAT	REBALANCE TO 3 BROS + DSL
Q11	SNAP	"ARCS" ON
Q12	SNAP	ROOM SWITCH OFF
Q13	SNAP	"ARCS" OUT WITH GUNSHOTS
Q14	SNAP	ROOM SWITCH ON
Q15	CHEAT	ADD FOR INTERROGATION D.R.
Q16	5 secs	FADE TO BLACKOUT

OTHER PROSCENIUM PLAY STYLES

I have used the box set realism style to illustrate the thought processes involved in designing a play. Drama, however, mostly bursts out of such a framework, not just of the box set framed by a proscenium arch, but of the proscenium itself. A later chapter discusses the implications of thrusting the stage beyond the confines of the proscenium. What happens when we take away the solid walls of a realistic room and substitute some sort of pure acting space with only simplified representational scenic elements to symbolise location and mood?

The first result for the lighting designer is freedom. Freedom from the tyranny of walls and ceilings which block the passage of light beams. Freedom from the hopelessness of trying to imitate the wonders of the natural light which stem from a single source reflected by the complex vibrant surfaces of a lighting environment. Freedom to use light in an expressive way to point and counterpoint the intellect and emotion of the drama. Ah, Wonderful Freedom!

But having gained this freedom, where do we find orientation? The window, the wall brackets, the restrictive walls were something to respond to, something to channel our thoughts. What now?

With a departure from reality acting increasingly becomes an exaggerated and/or simplified version of normal behaviour. Scenery becomes an exaggerated and/or simplified statement, using selected symbolic items from a real environment. Likewise, lighting becomes an exaggerated and/or simplified statement – essentially a clearer, more positive, light than the gently reflective, all pervading unobtrusive light of normal life.

Under these conditions there is likely to be greater emphasis on the use of light to create space by pulling it out of surrounding darkness. This will involve considerable emphasis on dimensional modelling from side and backlights. Such lighting styles are often best achieved by the 'four lights at ninety degrees' method rather than the three light method of paired fan-set face lights plus backlighting.

As we move away from naturalism, light cues can become more fluid. Windows, and the view through them, are the first things to be jettisoned on the flight from naturalism. Practical lamps may linger, but the resultant light need play scant attention to the logic of the source. Light cues can become free to happen for purely selective or emotive reasons.

What sort of key light(s)? Does the set suggest a directional key light? Or perhaps a series of directional keylights appropriate to individual scenes? Whatever the result of our thinking, the solution is likely to have two features. A strong positive lighting statement that the audience are immediately aware of; and a back-up rig, probably on the fan principle, that develops the light within the logic of the key source to project the actor to his audience.

It is now quite common to ignore masking on the proscenium stage and leave all the lighting equipment on view. Sometimes the structure of the rig is deliberately designed as part of the set, its shape often complimenting the form of that set. At other times a normal rig is just exposed: this is a positive style decision and when it is made, there is a strong case for exposing only the upstage bars which are most likely to include the positive key lamps. The mass of secondary fill equipment immediately behind the proscenium is perhaps best left hidden.

11
Lighting dance

Sculptural enhancement of the human figure is the primary requirement of lighting for dance. While dancers' expressions must be visible, it is with their limbs that they 'speak'. Therefore the entire body has to be made visible in a way which will maximise the three-dimensional quality of the dancer's movements and separate them from the surrounding environment.

For this reason most lights on the dance stage are focused either as downlights or crosslights. Very few are pointed upstage, either directly or on the diagonal angles of the fan settings commonly used in drama when eyes and teeth are such a priority for visibility.

Such a generalisation is, of course, to be modified by considerations of style. Classical ballets, particularly those with a strong narrative plot, are likely to require a softer, more frontal light than an abstract modern piece. Classical choreography tends to fill the stage: a dancer can traverse the entire stage with a very few steps. Therefore light is unlikely to be used selectively to any great extent other than perhaps a 'tightening' achieved by cheating down the edges. Some modern dance, on the other hand, uses complex movements by dancers in relatively static positions. Both classical and contemporary dance tend to utilise strong colour for atmosphere. For the classics this is often a romantic heightening of nature with the moon truly blue and the sun particularly golden.

Settings for dance very rarely include raised levels. Indeed there is a general need to provide as much clear space as possible. And lots of entrances are preferred – both to give a range of options (it is difficult to enter from where someone else has just made a leaping exit) and to simplify getting a lot of people simultaneously on or off. Multiple entrances are good news for lighting since they ensure that the sides of the stage are sufficiently open to allow the necessary positions for modelling lights.

Although large scenic pieces may be found in some classical ballet design, the great majority of dance takes place within a space bounded by backcloth and wings. Many modern dance companies have a standard setting of black wings and borders, an alternative of sky or blacks at the back, and a vinyl dance floor which may be black but is more likely to be white or grey. Cloths or, more likely, small scenic pieces may be used at the back. Bigger companies may also use wing flats as an alternative to blacks for some works in the repertoire.

This standardisation of the acting area enables considerable standardisation of not only the lighting rig but much of its focusing. This is fortunate from the lighting management point of view since most dance programmes, apart from the big three act classics, consist of three or four one-acters which are chosen in virtually any permutation from the total repertoire. Therefore the maximum changeover time between any two dance pieces in a performance is likely to be the fifteen minutes of a standard interval. This imposes a considerable discipline on the use of the lighting rig which is often organised in the following basic groups:

- Fixed focus and colour.
- Fixed focus but with remote colourchangers with fixed range of colours. (The four or five colours of semaphores and wheels is now expanded to the three dozen or so of scrollers).
- Fixed focus but allowed an interval colour change.
- Refocusable during intervals.
- Specials unalterably set for works in the current repertoire.

As already indicated, the fixed focus lights on the overhead spot bars are normally set as back, down and crosslights – very rarely on the diagonal. Downlights are particularly important in dance, both for their contribution to the modelling and for the way they colour the floor and help wash out dancer shadows which would otherwise be distracting on its untextured surface. Of the crosslighters on the bars, those at the extreme ends, known as the *pipe-ends*, are of particular value for modelling from a high angle. Frontal lighting from the auditorium is used very sparingly and mostly from positions to the side; many modern dance companies use virtually no foh.

Sidelighting is usually provided from low booms, rarely higher than about 12 or 14 ft, mounted on small castored trucks heavily weighted for stability. These can be moved up/down and on/off the stage according to the masking arrangements and are normally set tight to the masking legs, allowing a space for entrance between the boom and the next leg upstage. The lowest lights are known as *shin busters* because they not only light the shins but are potentially dangerous to dancers making exits. The lowest shin buster is often set to splash across the stage floor while the instrument immediately above clears the floor. Going up the boom, a series of horizontally set lights catch the dancer's bodies. Since dancers at the side of the stage will be close to the lights, wide angles and soft edges are required: fresnels are therefore often favoured. Vertical spread for dancers close to a side light may be improved by directional diffusers such as Rosco 104. Profile spots with break-up gobos, focused horizontally across the stage, can make an interesting contribution of chiaroscuro to the lighting palette since they do not show until the dancers pass through their beams. Colours may be changed easily on side lighting trucks, not only in the interval but during the performance.

Follow spots are sometimes used in classical ballet but a single frontal follow spot can be very flattening if it in any way approaches being a major source of light. If follow spotting is used there should be at least two, or preferably three, from angles appropriate to sculptural modelling. In modern dance, however, the follow spot is normally to be regarded as a special effect.

Dance is potentially one of the most exciting areas for lighting. The possibility of concentrating on modelling and atmosphere rather than detailed visibility for eyes and teeth allows light to make a particularly integrated contribution. The absence of scenery in the acting area reduces some elements of compromise and allows the lighting scope for maximum fluidity in creating the performance space. The absence of scenery also leaves a reasonably clear grid, allowing lighting equipment a better chance of placement where required, while the minimal use of foh removes many of the problems associated with getting good lighting positions within the restrictions of auditorium architecture. Dance companies often use quite extensive lighting rigs but a great deal can still be achieved on a low budget. Stands in the wings plus pipe ends and downlighters are the basics.

12
Lighting music theatre

Although such labels as opera and musical are still applied to theatre based on sung rather than spoken communication, the distinction between various performance forms has become increasingly blurred in recent years – both for new writing and in the way older works are presented. Indeed many productions of drama texts now involve so much music and choreographed movement that any division of our discussion into drama, dance and music theatre might be regarded as irrelevant. Nevertheless, while there is undoubtedly a large area where cross-fertilisation between forms is developing an integrated 'total theatre', there are still considerable differences between the lighting contribution made to mainstream drama, conventional opera and the various manifestations of what we usually refer to as the 'the musical'.

Any work of music theatre is a long way from realism: we tend to communicate with each other by speech rather than by singing duets. Yet, having established a musical format at the beginning of a performance, an audience quickly find musical communication to be quite normal, natural, and even realistic.

In the past, theatre used music, whether in the form of song or dance, as an addition to the spoken drama. The musical numbers were added as a commentary to the action, rather than as a means of carrying the action forward. Then the musical ensembles at the ends of the acts began to be part of the action. This spread to the duets, trios, and other ensemble pieces in the middle of the acts, until today, when most musicals aim to be completely through-composed, even reflective romantic solos carry the action forward.

Originally, there was little difference between opera and other forms of musical. In the first half of this century, the two went their own diverse ways – at least in Britain and America, although perhaps not entirely in central Europe where operetta was the popular form of the more lighthearted musical stage. In lighting terms, many differences are organisational: opera has to be played in repertoire because of the vocal demands on singers, whereas a musical can play for a continuous run.

MUSICALS

The principal difference between the average musical and the average play is *size*. The musical has more people and more scenes. This inevitably means more money. For lighting it means more instruments, more cues and more planning. And any cynic will tell you that, for all involved, it means more hysteria.

Style

So where do we start? Yes, no surprises, it's back to style. As always this grows out of the extent and manner of the departure from naturalism. Production style in a musical is strongly influenced by two decisions. Firstly, the extent to which the director is going to treat the musical numbers as an integral part of the show. Secondly, how the designer is going to deal with the diversity of scenic locations demanded by the script.

Musical Scenery

Pictorial scene painting is still very much alive in the world of the musical. Play designers, whether working in a naturalistic style or not, tend to build solid three-dimensional scenic units from strongly textured materials which require little assistance from paint. But an entire musical scene may still be painted on a canvas drop as big as the proscenium opening. The plots of many older musicals were constructed to alternate between full-stage scenes and front-cloth scenes. These front-cloths not only mask major scene changes, they allow time for costume changes for the chorus singers and dancers required for the full stage numbers.

Decorative Masking

To speed the flow from one scene to another, while minimising the number of crew required to handle the changes, most modern musical productions do not build complete scenes. They use the *decorative masking* principle where the stage has a permanent arrangement of wings, borders, and backcloth. This masking is not the conventional neutral surround of skeleton-set-drama, but a very positive pictorial masking, often decorated with a colourful motif or even based on a definite constructional idea such as elaborate trellis-work. For individual scenes, representational pieces stand, often island-like, within this masking surround. In the smallest-scale productions, these scenic pieces may be just small free-standing cutouts carried on from the side. As the shows grow more ambitious, they increase in size until ultimately they become so huge and heavy that powered assistance is required to move them on a special stage flooring criss-crossed with guiding tracks.

An Average Musical Setting?

Although there can be no standard scenic treatment, many of the possible approaches to the problem have enough common features to let us consider what might, for lighting purposes, be termed the average musical setting. The common denominator is the borders and wings approach which, whether permanent or not, is the most practical way of providing for a large acting area with the possibility of quick simultaneous entrances and exits by a large cast.

An Average Musical Lighting Style?

Whether or not the music numbers are an integrated part of the show, few musicals are carried continuously forward in music. A more normal pattern is still spoken dialogue alternating with musical numbers. When these musical numbers are a commentary interleaved between dialogue sections, different lighting styles are often used for the two types of scene. The dialogue scenes are enacted in lighting approximating to that of a naturalistic play, but, with 'cue for song', the lighting does a conscious contrasting change. One convention has soloists picked out by follow spots while the rest of the stage cheats down to a suitably coloured ambience. At the end of the musical number the light builds back to normal, often over the last few bars to support the climax, inevitably encouraging applause. There is a danger that the move from a contrasty light with follow spots into a general light coverage will drop the dramatic tension of the scene and, unless the follow spot is faded very discreetly and only after the lights are fully back to 'normal', the actor may even appear darker. For brash noisy numbers the light has to be built fully bright and given an even brighter 'bump' right at the end of the climax. (To make this bump possible, the lights can be subconsciously cheated down before the end of the number so that there is some intensity available for bumping back consciously to full.) A very atmospheric lighting for songs can give a feeling of anticlimax when the light returns to a speech style. So this is an area where great care in

timing has to be exercised: there have been many musical productions where abrupt changes in lighting and production
styles have destroyed the author's and composer's attempts to
write a show with a true marriage of words and music.

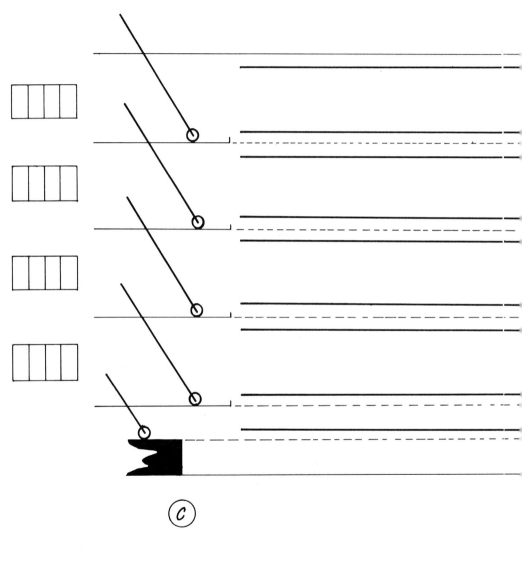

**Large scale musical
with extensive
lighting resources**

FOH A
Frontal actor bash
FOH B
Downstage cloths

FOH C & D
Downstage actor modelling
FOH E & F
Downstage fill

Bar 1
Downstage downlight
(Too close to false pros for lighting upstage)

Bar 2
Probably stack of at least two bars
General upstage fan
Specials for particular scenes
Downlights
Bar 3 & 4
Mainly downlight
Requirement for specials reduces upstage
Bar 5
Cloth lighting
Bar 2A, 3A, 4A
Height required to mask these bars means that a planned backlight becomes almost a downlight.
Bar 5A
Backlight
Perch Booms
Tight space but useful for side lighting busy downstage area.
Boom 1
Probably double-banked to light both across and upstage
Booms 2, 3, & 4
Mainly cross-lighting. Usually profiles to shutter-off specific pieces of scenery.
Boom 5
Profile to prevent spill on backcloth or cyclorama.
Ladders 1, 2 & 3
Alternative to booms or can be in addition to provide fresnel colour washes.
Ladders 4
Disaster if knocked – beams splash all over cyclorama.

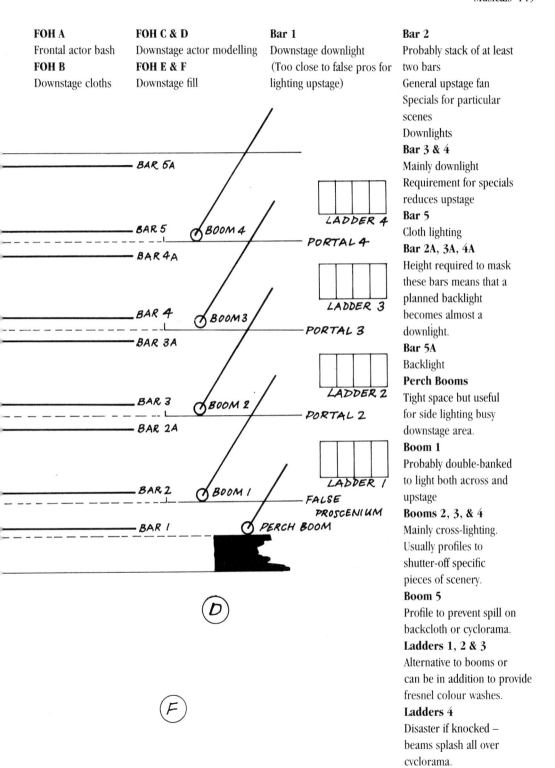

An Average Musical Lighting Rig?

Whatever way it is decided to use light in a particular production, there is likely to be a basic requirement to control the light within the following framework of possibilities:

- The facial clarity of naturalistic drama *and*
- the figure modelling of the dance *combined with*
- selective emphasis on appropriate scenic units *and*
- a wide range of ambience, possibly embracing the extreme limits of the colour spectrum.

Facial clarity tends to be required only towards the front of the stage. In the interests of establishing audience contact, important scenes tend to be played well forward: the only important upstage speeches are delivered from the tops of staircases, probably on entrance or exit. Facial clarity is only required for musical numbers if there are no follow spots. Traditionally, these musical numbers were delivered well downstage to be near the orchestra, but radio microphones plus fold-back loudspeakers have brought more freedom of movement to singers.

In many cases facial visibility for the dialogue scenes can be achieved from the foh and first spot bar positions, with a few lights on a midstage bar to face-light staircases and the like. These face lights use pale tints whereas the rest of the rig is in more positive colours. The bars will carry some spots to pick out scenic features but most of the remainder of the rig, whether from above or from the side, will be used to put colour and modelling into the chorus singers and dancers. Even in a modern musical, where the chorus may be individual characters rather than an anonymous mass, they tend to be used in the form of background dressing and are therefore more fun to light than the principals. If the chorus do have anything special to say or sing, they tend to come forward either as a mass or as individuals to deliver from the face-lit downstage area. For dance numbers, the sculptural modelling is increased by using a greater proportion of side light.

To soft light a painted front-cloth, there is nothing to beat the sources which are disaster for normal actor lighting: fresnels flat on from the front of the lowest balcony plus a touch of footlight.

The illustrations show the scope of typical plans for large and small resource musical shows. Over the entire stage area, provision is made for top and side lighting in at least two,

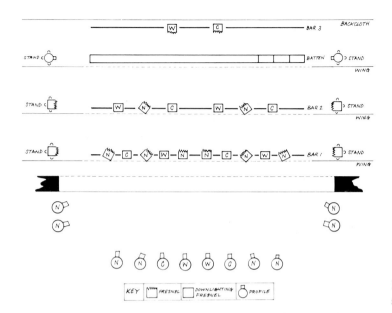

Musical using small
scale resources

preferably three colours. Using the strongest saturated colours from back and downlights, intermediate colours which are strong but have an incisive clarity from the sides, and neutrals from the front, we have a colour *palette* that offers considerable scope for the different requirements of song, dance and dialogue.

Practical Rigging

The best positions for the overhead bars are immediately upstage of the borders. The horizontal masking borders are often framed and bolted to their corresponding vertical masking legs to form solid *portals*. Thus the masking becomes a series of portals, rather like a series of prosceniums. Indeed the first portal is usually called the *false proscenium*. If the lighting bars are flown next to the portals, they are able to light upstage without spilling on the front of the next border. Also the lights are protected, to some extent, from being knocked by moving scenery.

This position is suitable for most normal purposes with the exception of *backlight* for which the ideal hanging position is immediately downstage of portals. Such bars require to be at a high dead to mask and care needs to be taken to ensure that light is not cut off by flown scenery hanging downstage of the bars: this can be a particular problem in theatres with low grids.

Where possible, side lighting is carried on booms screwed to the stage floor. Again, these booms should be fixed immediately upstage of the masking legs to allow their light to be angled slightly upstage and to keep them clear of scenery and actor movements. If scenery movements make booms impossible, the side lights may be hung on ladder-like frames, clear of the stage floor. This is reasonably satisfactory, although for dance it is usual to have some lower, horizontal, side lighting. It is, naturally, disastrous if a ladder is knocked during a scene change: the whole structure and its light beams will continue to swing throughout the following scene. For the small-scale show, lights on stands can be used. But they should be supervised by stage electricians since, apart from the risk of the equipment being knocked by scenery, it will probably be necessary to change the side lighting colours of a small rig between scenes or even cues.

THE GREAT AMERICAN BACKSTAGE MUSICAL: A BIG MUSICAL ON A SMALL SCALE

'Look kid, I don't say this every day of the week, but you're going places. You got class and you got what it takes.'

'Thanks Sylvia. But I happen to think that I can stick right here with Johnny and still get my name in lights.'

'If you stick right here with Johnny, the only way you'll get your name in lights is if you change it to Coco-Cola.'

This kind of dialogue will be very familiar to anyone who loves theatre as portrayed in the 'I'm gonna make you a star' type of Hollywood showbiz movie. Alas, they don't make 'em that way any more, but you can still catch a re-run on television.

The programme of *The Great American Backstage Musical* listed the scenes simply as *Place and Time: New York, London and the battlefields of Europe, 1939 to 1945.* This included such locations as backstage, onstage, the dressing rooms of tacky clubs and Broadway hits, tea at the Ritz and coffee at a soda fountain, entertaining the front line troops (direct hit, next scene a field hospital) etc, etc. All the normal stuff that epic musicals are made of. However this was the Regent Theatre – a cinema with no wings, no flys and a token stage.

But designer Robert Dein worked miracles of scenic statement. Two portals of black glossed scaffolding lined with black bolton sheeting framed one of the Regent's peculiarities, turning it into an asset. If a small stage happens to have an attractive

Backstage at *The Great American Backstage Musical* showing the upstage right lighting boom between a scaffolding portal and the ornamental balustrade which is a permanent feature of the Regent stage.

cast iron balustraded balcony running along the back wall and blocking off a significant part of the stage's depth, there is no point in ignoring it. It will not go away: you just have to use it. And so the balcony became many things. The miniature roll-up cloths for the club stage scenes were hung under it to convey smallness of scale. It became a cross-lit feature of the Ritz. It became the location of the Soda Fountain scene. It became a useful level for dry-ice tanks and flash-boxes. It was only hidden for the Broadway Spectacular scenes when a full height pair of silver lurex tabs made, by contrast, a very big statement.

Within this framework, small cut-outs, mini-trucks, and

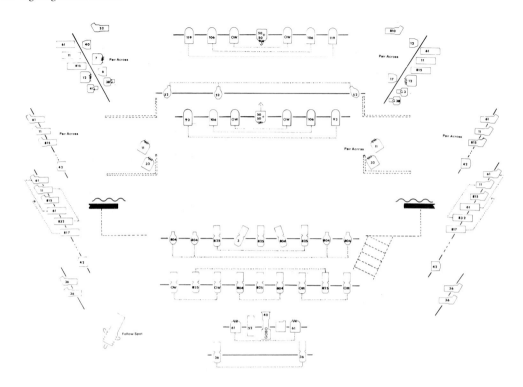

Lighting plan for *The Great American Backstage Musical*

	Pattern 264 (plan)	1 kW profile
	Pattern 264 (section)	1 kW profile
	Pattern 764	1 kW profile
	T spot	1 kW profile
	Pattern 23 (plan)	½ kW profile
	Pattern 23 (section)	½ kW profile
	Parblazer	1 kW (120 volt) sealed beam Par 64
	Pattern 750	1 kW beamlight
	Pattern 743	1 kW fresnel
	Pattern 123	½ kW profile
	Pattern 137	fotofloods random flashed for battle effect

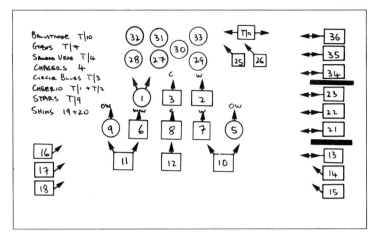

The **standard 1:25 scaled lighting layout plan** can be unwieldy during lighting, technical and dress rehearsals. However, the essential information can be condensed on to a standard 8in × 5in index card. A big show may use both sides but *The Great American Backstage Musical* fitted easily on to one side. The symbols for the coloured channels were drawn in red, blue or yellow.

essential furniture were used to suggest location. This scenery had to be small – there was little wing space to store it and, even with a cast of only six, an acting area of about 18ft by 16ft does not leave a great deal of room for lavish scenery.

There were three types of lighting required:

(1) Straight 'play' lighting for the dialogue scenes.
(2) Atmospheric treatment for the musical numbers.
(3) More exaggerated treatment of the musical numbers taking place on stages (the 'musicals within a musical').

The lighting was a 'scaled-down version of the type of rig used on big musicals. Pale natural tints from the front, strong colour from the sides, and really saturated colour from above and behind.

The Regent is so small that all face light has to come from the auditorium, but there are two ceiling bars over the stalls at a good face angle, together with another bar over the balcony and a pair of booms at the balcony sides giving a good fill. The stalls ceiling bars were focused straight in with no crossing. (Yes, perhaps a little flattening but in this particular show it was more important to keep the dialogue scenes tight with minimum light spill on the black portal frames.) On such a small stage there was little point in splitting left, centre and right (or even just left and right – for the one scene requiring this, there were a couple of specials) so the area was split into *inners* and *outers*, to give control of the degree of tightness of any particular scene. All these spots were profiles with pale tints.

The down and back lighting was provided by 1 kW PAR 64 units (120 volt in series pairs) giving high intensity from saturated near-primary colours and creating that depth-enhancing haze, characteristic of backlight in general and sealed-beam lights in particular.

The dialogue scenes were lit mainly from the front with just a low-level toning from above. The backstage working light scenes were rather harshly white, while other locations were given softer tinting. For musical numbers, side colour was added and the single follow spot used rather discreetly. For onstage 'musical within a musical' scenes, the colour became much more contrasty and the follow spot more obvious. And some obviously 'stagey' devices were introduced, such as chasers, dry-ice, flash-boxes, flashing photofloods, gobos and shin busting beamlights at floor level.

To provide a link with the movies, the show's credit titles were run on the Regent's cinema screen during the overture. This was achieved (at less expense than film and projectionist) by cross-fading a pair of 35mm carousels from a bar on the front of the balcony. This position, often omitted from new theatres because it would produce a bad (i.e. horizontal) face angle, can be very useful in a musical. Here it was vital for such jobs as picking up sparkle on the tabs and projecting a silhouette gobo during a radio announcement.

The house control was a 36-way Mini 2 which carried the main load, plus a temporary 12 way Mini 2 for the specials. The twin boards were handled by one (excellent) operator from an end-of-balcony control position. There was no conventional lighting rehearsal – the show was plotted by a fast pencil during a semi-dress stagger-through with the actors.

OPERA

I suggested earlier that opera was little different from other forms of music theatre except that it was played in repertoire. This, although essentially true, is something of a generalisation. Certainly, opera has the basic musical features of sheer size, exotic locations, and principal singers who do their stuff at the front of the stage to be near the orchestra. However the pace is generally slower with fewer but longer scenes. Any permanent masking tends to be functionally sombre rather than decorative. Some opera productions still adhere to the tradition of complete scene changes but permanent settings with minimal rearrangements are perhaps now more common.

The director of a play, and perhaps to a lesser extent, the director of a musical, has a considerable choice of style available. But the director of an opera has less freedom: the style is largely determined by the musical score. To go against the timing and atmosphere laid down by the composer is rarely easy and, even when possible, often disastrous. The lighting style also stems from the music. Quick buffo comedy requires the clarity of the straight play, while sustained romantic anguish flourishes in atmospheric backlights and crosslight. A great deal of opera is concerned with tragic happenings. Much of it takes place by moonlight, and even some of the daylight scenes are located far from the rays of the sun.

The colours are rarely extreme: the warms are the tints of the straight play, but the cools become bluer as the tragedy deepens and reality gives way to romanticism. All aspiring opera lighting designers carry steel blue filters in their knapsacks, and would do well to have sheets of the slate blues which flood the stage in cool blue yet bring a warmth to heroic cheeks.

Problems of repertoire changeovers are discussed in the next chapter.

LIGHT ENTERTAINMENT

There is a whole stratum of theatre which has no script and little rehearsal. There is often no designer and when there is a director, the role is likely to border on that of referee. The only document is a list, often written on the back of a box-office advertising card, known as *the running order*. This tends to be subject to last minute change. The word 'light' in the term 'light entertainment' has nothing to do with stage lighting. 'Light Entertainment' covers everything from variety to a reasonably large spectacular revue put together by inserting star personality acts into a framework of 'production numbers'.

Variety artistes have their own lighting plots, again usually written on the back of box-office cards. These plots use the terms 'full-up', 'red stage', 'blue stage', 'colours' and 'blackout'. This gives an idea of the atmospheric mood to be created around the artiste while visibility is taken care of by a follow spot. The practical way to deal with this situation is by using on-stage downlighters and crosslights in ambers, reds and blues – not primaries, just a selection of the more fruity, saturated colours. From the front some paler colours help the full-up and comedy scenes.

ROCK LIGHTING

For rock concerts, the lighting rig and loudspeaker stacks form the major features of the visual environment. The lights are normally rigged on truss formations which are free standing, the overhead sections being supported on the tower units by which they are hoisted into position. The standard lighting instrument is the parcan used in mass formations whose complex patterns make a strong visual impact. Symmetrical placing of colour filters ensures that the fronts of the parcans make a contribution to the design which adds to the pattern of the beams, often emphasised by the use of smoke. The essence of much rock lighting is its dynamic movement, achieved not only by flashing and sequencing from the control board, but also by the use of special spotlights which are either motorised to move or have associated motorised mirrors to divert their beams.

Many recent musicals have adopted some of the techniques of rock lighting, particularly when they have a music score in the rock idiom.

TRADE SHOWS

In recent years a whole new area of performance has developed out of the application of theatre staging techniques to such events as product launches and sales conferences.

Lighting is used to ensure that a company's products are revealed with dramatic effect in an atmosphere of maximum glamour. Budgets are high, often providing for large rigs with a proliferation of effects with lasers and smoke popular. Dancers and comedians are used to warm up the audience so that they are prepared to accept the managing director as a star whose speech is then presented with every showbiz device to enhance its credibility.

The large budgets of rock and trade shows provide funding for much of the lighting industry's research and development which would be difficult to support on the tight margins of traditional theatre.

13
Lighting thrust stages

Our discussion so far has been in terms of conventional proscenium stages. What happens when we bring the action forward through the proscenium arch towards the audience? There are varying degrees of doing this.

We can remove the proscenium arch altogether but still have the audience sitting in conventional rows facing an end stage. Lighting techniques remain the same, except that distinctions are somewhat blurred between what we traditionally call foh lights and on-stage lights.

We can keep the proscenium arch but push the stage out towards the audience in the form of an apron stage. Lighting again remains standard, although a lot of foh is required and there can be difficulty in getting good light positions, particularly as such aprons are often added to conventional proscenium stages.

New lighting problems arise as soon as the stage thrusts so far into the auditorium that members of the audience are seated on more than one side of the stage. With a small degree of thrust, the majority of the audience will sit facing the front of the stage in a conventional way, but a small proportion will view from the sides. As the degree of thrust increases, a larger proportion will have a side view. Ultimately the thrust will increase until we have total encirclement of stage by the audience: theatre-in-the-round.

What are these lighting problems? What are the basic differences in lighting such a thrust stage rather than a proscenium stage?

Some things are easier. Because the actor is closer to the audience, we need less light than would be required in a proscenium theatre of comparable size. And, because the audience are no longer looking at a framed picture, there is less problem with the possible flattening effect of front light: thrust acting is inherently sculptural. It is not only difficult to act in a small corner of the playing area of any thrust stage, particularly theatre-in-the-round, but it is contrary to the audience contact philosophies to which thrust staging is a response. So we are less likely to select areas.

Therefore, the primary requirements of thrust or arena lighting are *illumination* and *atmosphere*. Atmosphere is normally controlled in any theatrical situation by balancing:

(a) light and shade *and/or*

(b) colour.

Atmosphere is often the result of contrast between the extremes of light and no light – or, more likely, the balance between light and not-so-much light. In thrust staging, atmosphere by light and shade is difficult to achieve because of the differently balanced pictures that would be offered to different segments of the audience. Because front light for one section of the audience will be backlight for a second section and side light for a third, it is better to keep a fairly uniform intensity balance from all parts of the lighting compass. Atmosphere becomes a matter of colour balance between cool and warm. On small stages, it may be possible to use a control with two presets to make permanent balances in cool and warm colours respectively, and run the entire performance by changing the proportional mix of cool and warm masters according to the changing emotional needs of the play.

And so the key problem becomes the provision of illumination without light shining in the audience's eyes. The easy way would be to light vertically. Certainly such light does not go into the audience's eyes, but unfortunately neither does it reach the actor's eyes and this operates against the actor's ability to communicate. However, this is not quite such a major problem in a small theatre-in-the-round as it would be in a biggish conventional theatre, because the audience is closer to the actor and there can be considerable upward reflection from furnishings and the floor. But the message is not that vertical lights are ideal or even acceptable: it is that lights for an intimate thrust theatre can afford to be at a somewhat steeper

Vertical Light

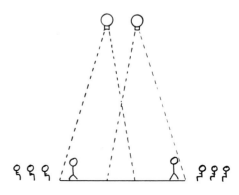

angle than would be advisable in more traditional theatre forms.

So where do we angle the light from? Light from positions *outside* the stage will light actors when they are on the edge of the acting area looking *outwards* to the audience. Light from positions *inside* the stage will light them on the edge of the acting area looking *inwards* (i.e. across the acting area) to the audience. So we need both.

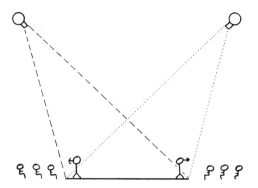 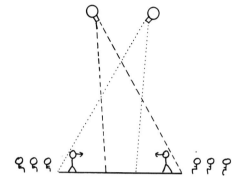

Light from positions *outside* the acting area will light actors on the edge of the acting area looking *outwards* to the audience.

Light from positions *inside* the acting area will light actors on the edge of the acting area looking *inwards* to the audience.

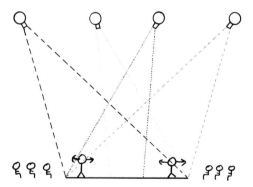

So we need both.

We have been looking at the problem in section. If we now consider it in plan, we find that, ideally, we need light from as many sides of the acting area as there are blocks of audience. With the complete audience encirclement of theatre-in-the-round, this will mean light from four sides. If audience are on three sides only, we should still have light from the fourth angle, otherwise one audience block will have a differently lit picture from the other two.

The plan shows basic one-colour acting area coverage for a small thrust stage. To give a complete two-colour atmospheric cover in warm and cool would require double the equipment, although it is possible to gain a lot of atmospheric control by using a basic cover for facial illumination and adjusting the colour tone with washes of positive colour from two or three hefty downlighters.

It is possible to reduce the number of lamps required by using only three angles on the actor: i.e. three lamps with a separation of 120° between lamps, rather than the four lamps with a 90° separation in the manner we have been discussing. I personally find balance much simpler to achieve with the four angle system; and balance is particularly important in theatre-in-the-round where all sections of the audience have a right to expect equality. But in a three-sided thrust form, it is almost inevitable that one audience block will be favoured by the actors and their director. My own personal preference is to aim for a four-angle coverage when the stage is enclosed by audience on all three sides. But I am prepared to drop down to three angles when budgeting for enough equipment for the inevitably large acting areas of thrust forms where the stage is not completely surrounded by audience and where some members of that audience are accorded the second class status which (and I stick my neck out) is inevitable in any theatre seating more than a couple of hundred or so, whether in proscenium or a more open form.

What of the practical physical problems of hanging lighting instruments for thrust stages? In large-scale purpose-built thrust theatres, accessible lighting bridges can be planned in the right positions to give the correct angle. But many thrust theatres are small-scale conversions of existing halls. Lights are often positioned high up on the walls, but this makes for too shallow an angle. Much more adaptable is a scaffold-pipe grid above the stage from which lights can be hung wherever required and ideal angles discovered by experiment. Even if the wall position is suitable, try to avoid the limitations of brackets: scaffolding bar is usually cheaper and certainly more adaptable.

Although profile spots give precise beam control and eliminate spill, I personally prefer fresnels or PCs with barndoors on small thrust stages. They join together more smoothly on the short throws which are often involved, and the inevitable auditorium spill of stray light is not a problem because thrust staging does not attempt to disguise the existence of audience as part of the scene.

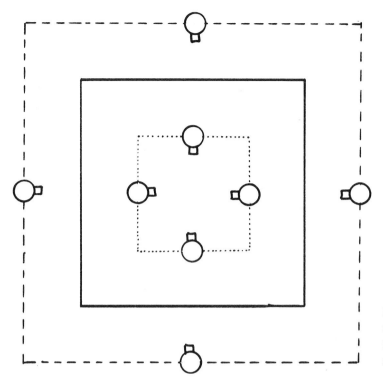

Plan showing light from the four sides in theatre-in-the-round.

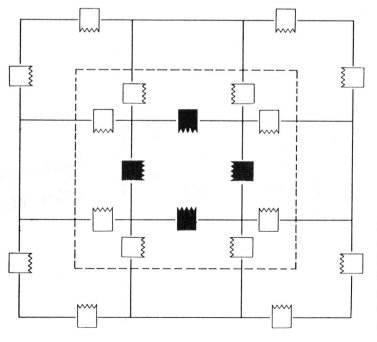

Plan showing a one-colour acting area for a small theatre-in-the-round, with an additional colour wash from four downlighters.

THE MULTI-PURPOSE SCHOOL HALL

To those faced with the problems of a multi-purpose school hall, I would suggest considering the possibility of abandoning the stage and thrusting the action into the body of the hall. Anyone who has worked on the average school stage knows what I mean by the problems. A letter-box stage with enough grey borders to fill a Palace of Varieties and a series of grey legs, shrunken unequally at the cleaners, and suspended on strange swivel devices which are supposed to adapt to various masking configurations but have an uncanny knack of swivelling to reveal all at dramatically unsuitable moments. The flat floor does nothing to help vision from anywhere beyond the first few seat rows, and, if the acoustic has been calculated at all, then that calculation has been briefed to deaden the noise of the multitude during assembly rituals. Because the hall has been designated multi-purpose, the onstage lighting has a large proportion of mini-floods which light the borders very brightly and the actors very little. In the better halls, there is no chandelier between the foh spots and the stage: even so, the proscenium opening is often wider than Drury Lane and the few spots on the side walls have some trouble in covering the stage. Where they do, the shadows are life size and fascinating — but hardly helpful in focusing attention on the dramatic action. Shall we thrust?

14
Lighting in repertoire

Most of the lighting techniques which we have been discussing assume that for each production we may choose and position instruments exactly where we require them – either by hanging a rig specifically designed for the production or by adapting a fixed rig with extensive additions and alterations. But this is only possible when there is to be a series of consecutive performances of the same production – whether the weekly run of standard touring, the month or so of a regional playhouse or the open-ended 'now and forever' which is the goal of Broadway and the West End.

However dance and opera companies always have a repertoire of several productions which they perform in an irregular rotation, usually with a daily changeover. Drama in much of central Europe is generally played in a repertoire system although elsewhere in the world, including most English speaking countries, the run of consecutive performances is normal.

Repertoire imposes restrictions on all staging departments. Changeover *time* is the limiting factor. Playing a different production each evening does not mean that the rest of the day is available for changeover. A repertoire theatre has new productions continually in rehearsal and the schedule has to provide for the stage being available for the technical preparation and dress rehearsal of these new works.

Because of the changeovers and the need for actors and orchestras to rest before evening performances, rehearsals are extended over a longer period than they would otherwise be, with a full stage rehearsal – technical or dress – taking two mornings rather than a full day.

Therefore the afternoon changeovers must be highly organised in their use of facilities. This implies a lighting rig where most instruments are hung in permanent positions, probably with the amount of refocusing restricted. The principal techniques used include:

Bridges

One approach, long standard in central Europe, is to make

instruments accessible by mounting them on bridges. The principal on-stage lighting position is a bridge – often a vertical stack of two or three levels – immediately inside the proscenium leaving only enough space for the house curtain and a couple of sets of flying lines. The bridge, although suspended to allow height alterations, is a firm structure on which crew can move during performances without causing vibrations which would shake the light beams. Associated with this horizontal bridge are a pair of vertical lighting towers which can be moved on and off stage. Consequently the bridge and tower structure is effectively an inner proscenium which provides a frame adjustable to the size and format required by any particular production. If desired the size and format can be changed between scenes. The bonus for lighting is that as the top comes down or the sides come in, they automatically bring the lighting instruments with them.

Although lights on upstage bars do not have access for focusing, the different heights of the platforms within the bridge structure provide the possibility of alternative lighting angles and central European fly towers are generally so high that flown scenery and masking borders do not obstruct the beams.

With lighting crew on the bridge and towers, instruments may be adjusted during quick scene changes and refocusing each one several times during a performance allows a relatively small number to cover a lot of situations. Bridges allow fast experiments during lighting rehearsals and are good for subtle following. Their drawback is the amount of space taken up and their tendency to push the action upstage: a problem in drama, although not so much in opera and dance.

Remotely Operated Instruments

With remotely focusable instruments, access is no longer required, making bridges and crew unnecessary although the basic lighting technique remains the same. Remotes are becoming common in upstage positions and seem likely to supplant bridges in the future.

Tapes

Many repertoire stages without bridges use variations of the 'tape grid' method. A new production is lit in the normal way, focusing from ladders. After plotting the cues, the scenery is struck and the positions of the light beams on the bare stage floor are recorded. To facilitate this, two canvas strips, usually known as 'tapes' are unrolled on the stage, one up and downstage on the centreline and the other across the stage on the setting line. The crossing point is zero and the tapes are marked with a numerical scale, prefixed L or R for left and right across the stage and + or − for upstage and downstage of the setting line. This provides a grid reference for each light beam's floor position. Notes can be made about edge shape and quality, perhaps accompanied by a drawing which, in conjunction with a record of focus knob positions, allows for considerable repeat accuracy.

It may be necessary to make final adjustments to a few instruments after the scenery has been set, particularly those highlighting a scenic feature, or perhaps narrowly missing scenery. But the majority of the focusing is accomplished very quickly since ladders can be moved rapidly on a flat stage free of scenery. By scheduling staggered meal breaks, the changeover work of the lighting and scenic crews can be integrated. If a grid is marked on the safety curtain, further time can be saved, since the foh can be focused while the curtain is down and the scenic fit-up continues behind. It may even be possible to focus while the orchestra rehearse.

Control

As noted when discussing control systems, boards for repertoire theatres are equipped with secondary memories to provide library storage. In early systems tape was sometimes used but disc is now standard. As part of the daily preparation for a repertoire performance the appropriate disc is used to programme the board's primary memory. Once the focus is complete and the scenery in position, as many cues states as possible are checked through – a quick process using a sequential push – so that intensity adjustments due to new lamps, cleaned lenses, minor focus variations, etc. may be made. These are memorised for today's performance only: for each subsequent performance the starting point is the master disc. Several copies of the master discs are, of course, kept under appropriate security procedures.

Repertoire Touring

The tape system is also used for touring, particularly by opera companies, although particular care is required in balancing memories because variations in stage dimensions and facilities mean that scenery can rarely be placed in identical positions in each theatre. Although the onstage lighting positions can be virtually identical each week, the foh will vary widely. However if the stage rig is toured with its own board, the theatre's own foh, on the house board, can be added quickly and balanced with the basic pictures already plotted within the touring board.

Many touring theatres in the United States feed their foh through a plug and socket panel system at the side of the stage. This makes it easy to divert any selected foh channels to a touring board. This would seem to be a practice which could with advantage become more universal.

Rigging

Fast efficient rigging, whether for repertoire or on tour, is essential for time saving. Traditional theatre is benefiting from adopting techniques used for the one night stand rock tours where sections of trussing complete with instruments and multi-connection sockets have simplified the rigging process – both for touring and for hanging extra lighting bars or trusses during rep changeovers.

The Future

New technology in rigging and remote focusing are combining with design discipline to reduce changeover times yet offer lighting with less compromise than has hitherto been unavoidable in repertoire situations.

15
Computer aided lighting design

Video screens play an ever increasing role in many aspects of our lives. The VDU is well established in stage lighting as the standard method of displaying operational information on lighting control desks, particularly channel levels and cue progress. Now the personal computer is becoming essential support for both lighting management and lighting design.

Lighting Management

Several software programmes have been written to aid management of the lighting process, particularly in organising paperwork, keeping it up-to-date and printing it out. Instruments, accessories and filters are not only listed but may be checked against stocks to calculate instant information on how much is left or will need to be acquired.

With computer drawing systems, instrument symbols can be positioned as required on the drawing and the usual data such as colour, channel number, gobo, etc. entered. The software enables various listings to be produced direct from the plan in the computer.

Software is also available to track the progress of each light in each cue, with instant information displayed on screen or in print. This information may be sorted by whatever category is most useful to the design team at any particular phase of the lighting process, whether before, during or between rehearsals. This can include keeping track of the channels which are in use or changing. Developments in remotely focusable spotlights will result in even more information to be kept track of during lighting sessions and subsequent rehearsals. With big rigs, pencil and paper are just not fast enough to keep the information up-to-date and accessible.

Information access will be further improved when manufacturers offer their catalogues in the form of computer software, either on discs or by direct delivery through the electronic mailbox facility on the personal computer which is already as standard a part of a lighting designer's work station as desk and drawing board.

Lighting Design

Most of these lighting management techniques use information technology to speed up processes which have hitherto been done manually. The end product is virtually the same paperwork as that formerly produced by laborious writing. However, computer aided design also offers the possibility of factual help with decisions which have traditionally had to be made on a basis which included a large element of guesswork.

Stage plans and auditorium sightlines for most British theatres are stored on disc for a system called *Modelbox* which has a software programme enabling a scene model to be viewed from various angles. In addition to checking audience sightlines for a particular auditorium, it is possible to discover the scope offered by various lighting positions, including follow spots.

Of particular interest is the possibility of assessing the effects of various lighting angles by manipulating a dynamic graphic video display. Computers can be programmed to look at a cross-section of the stage in terms of the interaction of beam angle, throw and spread. These programmes hold the characteristics of many commonly used spotlights, including their beam angles and the amount of illumination for any given throw distance. Alternatively this information may be keyed in for any particular piece of equipment. The essence of the operation is the same as using standard drawing techniques. If we know any two of beam angle, throw distance and spread, we can find the third. We can also experiment, simply and visually, by using the computer's cursor to move the spotlight position around the theatre and move the actor up and downstage while keying in alternative beam angles for the spotlight to be used. The early programmes were two dimensional, but systems are now able to provide a three dimensional graphic view of the beams and the shadows they cast. Since the screen displays an isometric drawing which changes automatically and immediately in response to movements of the cursor, these programmes offer considerable assistance to the lighting designer in agonising over the best positions for instruments.

Modelbox Autolight

Autolight is an example of the software packages which are moving lighting design from slow drawing board to fast video screen, not only speeding up routine tasks but allowing the consequences of critical design decisions to be discovered instantly.

When positioning spotlights, various interacting factors have to be weighed against each other to establish the best compromise. At what angle will the light from a particular position hit an actor at a particular point on the stage? Will it throw an awkward shadow? How big an area will result from different beam angles? What shape of beam splodge will be thrown on the floor from this oblique angle? Or that one? Autolight demonstrates on the screen.

The screen accommodates any size of rig plan and you zoom in and out of various sections as you work on them, expanding the images to a comfortable size for eyeballing. Instrument symbol positions are manipulated by editing routines which allow a plan to be developed, altered and amended, working on the lights singly or in groups, moving them around and gradually adding data (filters, gobos, channel, etc.) as decisions are made. A decision to swop the fresnels on bar three for profiles, or change all the Silhouettes in the rig to Cantatas is a matter of stroking the keys and watching it happen before your very eyes. Autolight has learned such fundamentals as not putting gobos in fresnels or irises in parcans and knows the characteristics of specified instruments: it will, for example, refuse instructions to demonstrate a 30° beam angle from a Cantata 11/26. While developing the design in plan, you can take an instant look in section at the beam of any light, with the option of having an actor or piece of scenery in position.

When completed, any lighting plan becomes the master source of information for the practical realisation of the design. Listings are required in many formats in order to prepare equipment and accessories. The traditional way is time consuming and prone to error: it is very easy for eyes and brains to miscount filters, irises and hook clamps on a big plan, but this is just the sort of work that computers excel at. Autolight generates all the obvious paperwork from equipment schedules to filter lists and, since its database includes weights, it will calculate flying loads on request. The capability to prepare a carnet from a plan is an indication of the machine's comprehensive management facilities. In addition to being displayed on the screen or printed out, these lists can be added to the drawing.

As far as 1999 and beyond is concerned, it does not take much of a crystal ball to predict that computer aided lighting

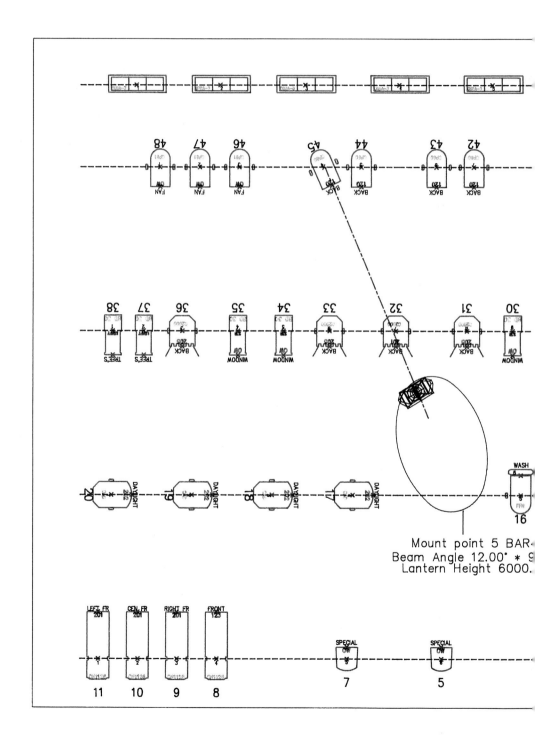

Mount point 5 BAR-
Beam Angle 12.00° * 9
Lantern Height 6000.

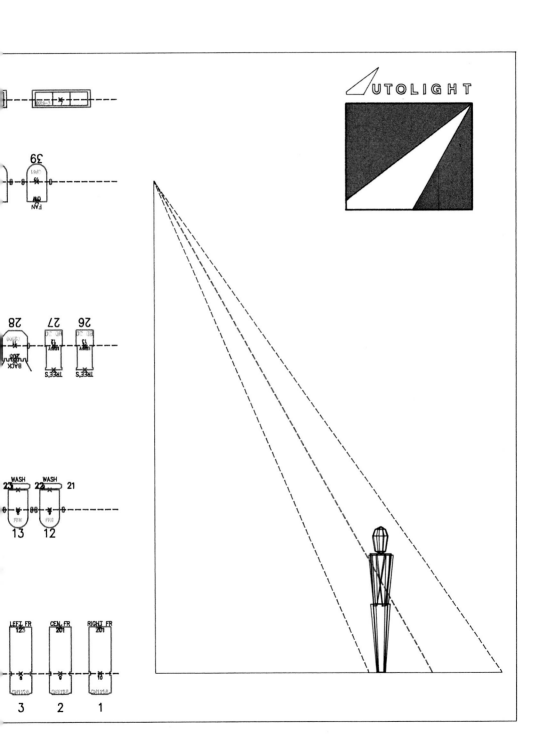

design can start dreaming about links with computer aided showlight manufacture. Autolight uses hardware which is related to the Graphic Tablet option on Arri control desks. It is not difficult to foresee design computers talking directly to control desks – and focusing lights!

Projection Design

A major problem in the use of projection is visualising and demonstrating within the set model how the projected images will look. Graphic design computers offer an aid. Using a video camera, the set model and all the proposed artwork for the projections are filed in the computer memory. The set is then displayed on the VDU and the projections superimposed one by one on the screen area. The computer's programme allows the projections to be scaled and cropped experimentally until the desired effect is achieved. By enabling the slides to be prepared accurately and advance decisions made by the production team as to sequence and cueing, considerable technical rehearsal time can be saved in the theatre.

Benefits and Limitations

Techniques such as these are just an indication of the technology that is being developed to aid the lighting process. However, it is important to remember that a computer is merely a device to remove some of the grind and guesswork from the craft to allow maximum concentration on the art. A computer can only make logical decisions, whereas art depends on illogical decisions made from the soul.

16
Square one

In the old days, standard stage lighting was a straightforward business of flat colour washes. Throughout the ages, there have been occasional focusable systems using complex rigs of candle wicks, oil lamps or gas mantles. But until quite recently, a lot of lighting consisted of washes from battens, footlights and wing floods.

Now this may not have been selective or sculptural, and it was only crudely atmospheric – but it was *quick*.

Modern spotlighting equipment can produce some splendid lighting, but takes time to prepare. This time can be made available when there are to be several consecutive performances, but such theatre is the tip of a huge iceberg of stage lighting users. Where is lighting time to be found in the multipurpose hall for the one-night-stand play, for the variety bill, for the end of term prize giving, for the symphony concert, for the . . . ?

In a situation which demands everything from bright white shadowless illumination for music stands to colour subtleties which will give a clean presentation of a no-scenery production, we rightly recoil from an installation of flooding equipment. In offering a good spotlight rig to such a stage, we are making available a *possibility* of good lighting – but a possibility that can only be realised with the expenditure of time and experience. In the average situation on such a stage, this time/experience may only be possessed by one drama group who will achieve marvels, but, after their last performance, will leave the equipment with specialised settings totally useless for other functions.

The joy of floodlighting was its 'back to square one approach'. It was not (indeed it could not be) angled or focused: you just hung it up, plugged it in and it was ready to produce all the lighting that it was capable of producing by just juggling with the dimmers.

It is this 'back to square one' that we should attempt to apply to the lighting of the multi-use stage. A standard approach to the problem has been to place a number of floods among the spots on the principle that, no matter how the spots are set, if you turn on the floods you will get some sort of light for the mayor's speech. Unfortunately these floods tend to throw more light on to the adjacent borders than on to His Worship.

Therefore, I would like to suggest that multi-use stages should have a *square one* setting for their equipment. There should be little or no restriction on the movement or focusing of the lighting instruments by specific users when time is available. *But*, after use, each one must be returned to its square one position, colour, and setting.

Variety will require its traditional red, white and blue approach. Plays are likely to call for more subtle facial coverage in warm and cool, while basic selectivity on a small stage with bad sightlines often boils down to a concentration of action and audience attention by 'taking down the edges'. An orchestral concert requires white vertical downlight and prize-giving is basically the same plus enough foh to help us see the platform party's faces without dazzling them.

A square one lighting rig

A possible way in which this square one approach might be adopted is suggested in the following lighting rig. As with every

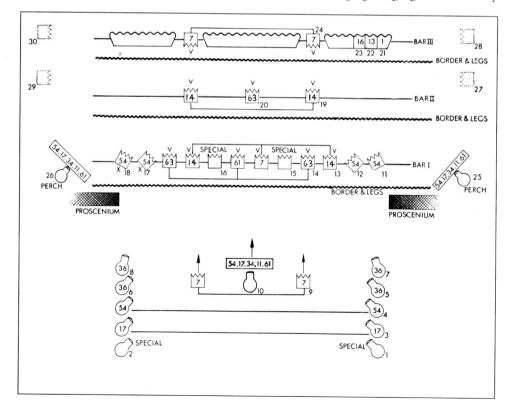

Circuit	Location	Lantern	Colour	Focusing
1	Auditorium side wall	Profile	Optional	Special
2		,,	,,	,,
3		2 × Profile	17	Centre Downstage
4		,,	54	,, ,,
5		Profile	36	Right Downstage
6		,,	36	Left Downstage
7		,,	36	Left Downstage
8		,,	36	Right Downstage
9	Auditorium Centre	2 × Fresnel	7	Flood Downstage
10		Profile	Colour Wheel	Centre Downstage
11	Bar I	Fresnel	54	Upstage Left & Centre
12		,,	54	Upstage Right & Centre
13		3 × Fresnel	7 & 14	Vertical
14		,,	61 & 63	,,
15		Fresnel	Optional	Special
16		,,	,,	,,
17		Fresnel	54	Upstage Left & Centre
18		,,	54	Upstage Right & Centre
19	Bar II	2 × Fresnel	14	Vertical
20		Fresnel	63	,,
21	Bar III	Batten	1	Flood Backcloth
22		,,	13	,, ,,
23		,,	16	,, ,,
24		2 × Fresnel	7	Vertical & Downstage
25	Perch	Profile	Colour Wheel	Across Stage
26		,,	,, ,,	,, ,,
27	Dips		For accessory and special lighting	
28				
29				
30				

Key to square one lighting rig

N.B. 'Left' and 'Right' refer to actors' left and right

other rig in this book, it is not put forward as *the* ideal, but as *a* possibility to stimulate ideas.

The test of such a rig will be whether users can come on stage half-an-hour before curtain up and get some reasonably appropriate lighting.

TYPICAL BASIC SQUARE ONE RIG

Thirty control channels of 2.4 kW maximum. For smaller stages, the units would be rated at 500 or 650 watt. As the stage increases in size, certain units could be progressively uprated to 1 or 1.2 kW. The colour numbers are Cinemoid. (Prefixing with a 4 for Strand, and a 1 for Lee will usually give similar colours.)

Foh – Sides

A pair of profile spots (54-rose) cover downstage centre in warm, and a pair of profiles (17-steel) cover the same area in cool. Four profile spots pick up the corners in a neutral colour (36-lavender) which blends in both warm and cool situations. One special each side may be focused as required.

Foh – Centre

Because the side walls in such halls are usually too far to the side in relation to the proscenium, it is desirable that some form of 'fill' light is provided from a central ceiling position close to the stage. Such positions often have access problems, but this has become easier with longer-life halogen lamps. The suggestion is a pair of fresnels (07-pink) to flood the entire stage front, and a profile spot with colour changer, focused to centre stage.

On Stage – Bar One

Three fresnels in pink/red (07 in centre, 14 at sides) are focused vertically downwards to produce a wash of warm light on the stage but not on the borders. Three fresnels do the same thing in blue (61 in centre, 63 at sides). Four profiles flood across the stage in a face-lighting wash. Two specials may be focused as required.

On Stage – Bar Two

A pair of down-lighting fresnels in ruby red (14) and one in blue (63).

On Stage – Bar Two

Three sections of 3-colour batten to flood backcloths, drapes, etc. A pair of downlighting (and slightly backlighting) fresnels in pink (07).

On Stage Side Lighting

One profile spot each side with colour changer, focused across the front of the stage. Four 'dip' plugs available for extra equipment.

METHOD OF USING

Plays

(In the following priority subject to time available.) Use basic cover circuits 3 to 12 inclusive, 17 and 28, 25 and 26. Focus 27 to 30 as keys (windows etc.). Focus 15 and 16. Reset 13 and 14 to face-lighting angles and re-colour them with paler filters. Ditto for 19 and 20. Focus 1 and 2. Rearrange as much of the installation as time permits to the play's special requirements – remembering to allow time to set it back to square one afterwards.

Variety

Basic red cover   – circuits 9, 13, 19, 24.
Basic blue cover   – 14 and 20.
Colour variations   – 10, 25, 26, 21, 22, 23.
Full-up   – Add 4 to 8, 11, 12, 17, 18.
Cross lighting from spots on stands (27 to 30) would add interest.

Rock and Pop

Put saturated colours into circuits 1, 2, 16 and possibly 17–30.

Orchestral Concerts

Take colours out of 13, 14, 19, 20, 24 and the resultant wash of white downlight should light the music without shining in the players' eyes.

Speechmaking

Take the colours out of 14 and 20. Possibly warm up with a

touch of 13, 19 and 24. Use as much foh (particularly circuits 9 and 12) as you dare without incurring the chair's displeasure. *And when you have finished tonight's show – set it all back to square one.*

A FLEXIBLE MULTI-PURPOSE RIG

A bigger multi-purpose rig offers the possibility of providing for a greater degree of flexibility without resetting. A good approach is to include enough parcans to cover the stage with an overall downlighting wash. Without filters, these parcans will give a good white light for music reading – indeed it might be too bright and need a little check down on the dimmers. With saturated, near primary colours, the parcans will give the positive colour mixes required for most kinds of musical production. This will enable the foh profiles and the spot bar focus spots to be 'square one' set for a general face coverage, warm and cool. The spot bar profiles are basically intended for specials, and if there is a reasonable stock of instruments available for dips, the side lighting could normally be left in position, with the downstage possibly on perch booms and the upstage on ladders.

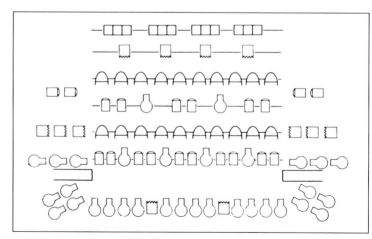

A flexible multipurpose rig

17
Projection and effects

Painting or photographing a scene on a slide for projection is neither an easy nor a cheap substitute for solid scenery. If projection is embarked upon it must be as a production style, probably because the script demands a wide range of instantly changeable locations and/or the luminous quality of a projected image is appropriate. Projection is often referred to as 'back projection' but, unless we use 35 mm carousel type projectors (see overleaf), there is rarely enough stage depth to project on to the screen from behind. Standard projection is more frequently on to the front of the screen and since such projection normally has to be at an oblique angle, the slides need to be specially prepared to counteract the distortion introduced by the angled throw. Scene projectors have special optical systems to produce an even light over the slide area and there are special cooling arrangements, usually involving fans and heat resistant glasses, to protect these optics and the slide. It is difficult to get enough projected brightness to balance with the actor light, and so scenic projectors tend to be physically big, the more powerful ones using discharge lamp sources. These use slides up to 24cm square which can be hand-painted as an alternative to photography.

Anyone contemplating projection on the smaller stage would do well to devise a projection style using standard 35mm magazine projectors such as the Kodak Carousel. These are not suitable for covering an entire backcloth, but exciting things can be done by incorporating a screen – or a series of screens – in a non-naturalistic setting. These screens can often be angled towards the projector to make correction against distortion unnecessary, and the projectors are small enough to conceal within the set. 35mm slide material is cheap and easy to prepare with a standard camera, and experiments can be carried out in the kitchen at home.

Even the biggest stages employ the 35mm carousel. The total picture to fill the screen is composed by joining a series of individual images from a bank of several carousel projectors. A 'grid' of nine is common, in three rows of three. Doubling up to

The **Pani BP4** with a 4 kW HMI discharge lamp is the international standard instrument for high intensity scenic projection in large theatres and opera houses. (An even brighter 6 kW BP6 is now available.)

The **Kodak Carousel** is probably the most versatile unit available for image projection. The *Lightworks Daylight Slide Projector* is an adaptation of the Carousel, using a 400 watt MSR projection lamp to double the normal screen brightness.

allow cross-fading between pictures makes a total of eighteen. A computer controls the crossfades between the projectors and advances the slide magazines. Since all the projectors can be individually faded, combination into a single total picture is just one of the possibilities. Sequential changing of individual projectors can be used to support a documentary or narrative production style. Images may be built up from fragments or given a feeling of movement by flip-flopping backwards and forwards between slightly displaced pictures of the same subject. Apart from the obvious production flexibility of such a system, it has technical advantages in that carousels placed behind a screen not only require a very short throw distance but, because projection is straight on rather than at an angle, predistortion of the slide is not required. Although the detailed movements of the sequences are memorised in the computer, an operator starts each part of the sequence to coordinate with the actors' timing. Since the carousels can hold many slides, a much more fluid projection system is possible than with conventional scenic projectors which until recently depended on hand-changing of slides.

PROJECTION SCREENS

Of almost overriding importance in the use of projection is the surface that the image falls upon. The best images are produced on special projection sheeting which is available in different types of material according to whether the projection is to be from the front, from the rear, or both. A major problem with screens is that they tend to look like screens and when there is no projected image they look like blank screens. Black rear projection screen produces good high contrast images and becomes inconspicuous when not lit. However, even when a screen has a matt surface there is a tendency to shine a little and to proclaim itself as a screen. One possibility is to hang a black open-meshed gauze in front of the screen and perhaps even paint it lightly with dyes. A black projection screen can also be back lit as a good sky.

When using a translucent screen (black or pale grey-blue) as a skycloth, smooth lighting coverage is obtained by hanging floods immediately upstage of the skycloth and bouncing their light from a plain white reflector cloth. With the light source between screen and bouncer, no light spills downstage and so particularly clean silhouettes can be obtained against the sky.

A projection screen need not fill the stage: part of the scene can be designed to transform into a screen when required. Or, if the image is non-realistic, it may make its impact by being projected on to the scene – projected textures on to real textures can be visually exciting. There have been screens composed of neutral walls with a series of various sized doors: a window is projected which then opens and someone looks out, but in the next scene a door may be projected which opens for an actor to walk through etc. Projection screen can be cut into strips so that actors may walk through the projected image; in its most sophisticated form slit rubber has been used, so that the screen image immediately springs closed and the actor seems to have appeared by magic. Projection has many possibilities if we think of it as another imaginative tool for the stage, not as an alternative to construction and paint.

SHADOW PROJECTION

This type of projection is often called *Linnebach*, after its pioneer. The picture is painted on a large piece of rigid transparent material such as perspex. The light source is a lamp in a black box without lenses or reflector. A separate stand is required for the large slide as the distance between source and slide varies considerably with the throw distance to the screen. The system works best for rather impressionistic subjects, and the whole process, including angular distortion of the painting, is best carried out on an experimental basis. Fortunately the size of the 'art-work' makes such experiment relatively easy.

GAUZES

Gauzes can create some of theatre's most beautiful magic. The principle is that, if we light only the front of the gauze, we will see only the picture painted on the gauze. But if we fade out this front light and build light on the scene behind, the gauze will become transparent and its picture will disappear.

There are two basic forms of gauze. One, often called English or transformation gauze, is rather like net and has more holes than thread. The other, American or hansen, gauze is thicker and has a woven texture with more thread than holes. Choice depends upon which picture is more important: the front or the dissolve. If we have a long scene in front followed by a short one behind, then the thicker woven gauze is better.

Front lighting for gauzes is ideally from sides and top, skimming along the surface of the gauze. It is therefore very important that the gauze hangs without creases. Straight-on frontal lighting will tend to go through the holes to reveal the scene behind. Very often, a black cloth is hung behind the gauze to allow actors to get into position under worklight.

To make a dissolve (sometimes known as a bleed) work properly, careful timing is essential. The sequence is usually:

Working light out
Blacks fly away
Build light behind ⎫
Fade light in front ⎬ possibly overlap
Fly gauze away
Add front light to main scene.

Most dissolve failures are the result of the director allowing insufficient time for the sequence to be properly paced.

Gauze is often used in non-transformation situations. As an alternative to canvas for painted backcloths, it can provide an interesting lighting texture, particularly for rather impressionistic vistas. A plain gauze hung in front of a backcloth or cyclorama is sometimes used to give a softening effect.

EFFECTS

I hope that the point has been made, and is being rammed home, that lighting must be an integral part of the production. This is especially true of effects – there is nothing like a display of drifting cloud, falling snow, or excessive forked lightning to distract an audience from contact with actors and script. Such goings-on must stem naturally from the production: they must never be grafted on just to decorate or enliven the proceedings.

Moving Effects

Moving effects attachments, usually in the form of a motor-driven disc, can be fitted to the front of scenic projectors. Several varieties of cloud are obtainable, and there are flames, rain, snow, waves, running water, etc. These effects usually look at their best when slightly out of focus. A fuzzy impression can often look more real than a hard accurate picture: *experiment!* Depth to a moving projection usually comes from superimposing several machines with slightly different focuses.

Traditional effects projections usually produce a picture of the actual effect. For production purposes, it is often more interesting to show not the actual phenomenon but the light that it casts. Thus a flickering light is often more convincing than a

CCT Starlette 2.5 kW
Effects spot with moving
effect

picture of the flames themselves, and shimmering light reflected off water conveys more than a picture of the water itself. Fire light can shimmer by waving a flag of fabric strips; this requires a particularly conscientious and sensitive operator. Water can shimmer by bouncing light off a reflective tray of water. But a more reliable (and less messy) way is to use a motorised flicker wheel. The traditional model includes a break-up glass and fits on to the front of a fresnel and becomes flame or water (clear or stagnant) by selection of an appropriate colour filter. Newer flicker wheels fit profile spots allowing a choice of appropriate gobo. Devices are now available to rotate gobos by variable speed motors or to 'yo-yo' a pair of gobos with a reciprocating motion.

Lasers

Lasers can be programmed to produce three dimensional images which hover in the air with a unique luminous quality. Their dynamic wave patterns, such as undulations and perspective tunnels, are particularly effective as are the darting beams produced by reflecting off a sequence of mirrors. The low powered lasers used in theatre require some smoke in the

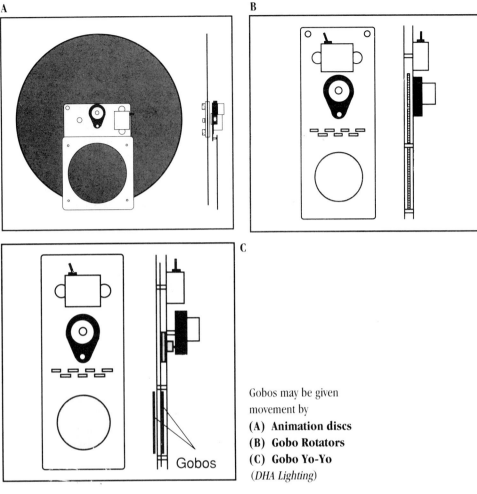

A

B

C

Gobos

Gobos may be given
movement by
(A) Animation discs
(B) Gobo Rotators
(C) Gobo Yo-Yo
(*DHA Lighting*)

air plus careful balancing of the other light if they are to register
to maximum effect. Lasers are expensive and dangerous: they
should only be installed and operated by laser specialists.

Psychedelics

Some of the extreme moving light effects are perhaps closer to
discotheque than stage. However, I remember a splendid production of Midsummer Night's Dream which made extensive
use of colours constantly breaking up and dissolving, by means
of moving prisms. Oil and water mixtures may be used with
dyes and filters to produce interesting random colour pictures.

Lightning

A very high percentage of the operatic repertoire calls for

heavenly intervention in the form of lightning. There are two forms — *fork* and *sheet*. Fork lightning is a projection: either a slide in a conventional projector or a gobo cut-out in a profile spot. In either case, the flashing is best done by a shutter or a piece of hand-held card, because the build and decay time of a lamp filament slows down the flash time if we make and break the electrical supply. However, any forked lighting is better with an operator because the fork should be moved to a different part of the sky for each lightning burst.

Sheet lightning is just a rapid series of flashes of intense white light, and the simplest lamp to flash is the over-run photographic lamp known as a Photoflood. This is the only type of tungsten lamp with a convincingly fast on and off. When flashing sheet lightning, beware showing up the stage masking arrangements in silhouette. The best place for sheet lightning is probably behind the groundrow at the bottom of the sky. A number of electronic flash devices are available. The simpler ones give a short intensive flash, but with a regularity related to the speed of re-charging. True lightning has an irregular rhythm for which programmable units are becoming available.

Strobes

Stroboscopes give a fast series of very short light flashes. Under this light, action appears to be frozen into series of jerky movements similar to early silent movies. The effect must be used sparingly, for it can induce sickness or even fits in members of the audience. For this reason, some licensing authorities insist that flash rates do not exceed eight per second.

Flashing and Chasing

Modern control technology simplifies the flashing and automatic sequencing of lights into patterns such as those where a series of lights appears to 'run' or 'chase'. Even quite simple control desks now have these capabilities, either incorporated in the desk or available as an add-on unit. The use of such light movements has become standard practice in popular music presentations and some of the techniques have been carried over into stage musicals. They can be very effective for musical numbers with a strong rhythmic beat if used sparingly: like everything else, over-use quickly blunts the impact of the effect.

Black Light

Certain materials will fluoresce under ultra violet (UV) light. As pure UV is a harmful radiation, special lamps, with filtering incorporated in the glass, must be used for stage UV. The easiest type to use is the 4ft UV fluorescent tube. For the best results, everything should be black except the bits which are treated to fluoresce. Fabrics which react to UV are available, as are paints and dyes. Materials which have been washed in certain detergents tend to fluoresce.

The most common use of UV is the type of pantomime underwater scene where UV light is the only light source on an otherwise blacked-out stage. The most sophisticated use is in the Black Theatre of Prague, where a combination of UV and a little careful directional light from the wings is used to sustain an entire evening's entertainment.

Fibre Optics

The smallest available points of light are those at the ends of optical fibres. The fibres may be fed to the rear of a piece of scenery and terminated in tiny holes to make line patterns from dots of light. The individual tails are grouped into a harness and led back to a unit where light is focused on to the end of the fibres by a special heat filtering reflector. A rotating colour wheel provides the possibility of changing colours. Fibre optics are particularly effective for skycloths where they have supplanted the traditional pea-bulbs. The fibres can be terminated on the black skycloth in random order or in the formation of specific constellations. With realistic skys, the use of two almost similar steels alternating in the colour wheel will give a convincing twinkle.

Smoke and Mist

No type of smoke which produces acrid fumes is acceptable for stage use. *Smoke* to disperse through the atmosphere is produced by smoke generators which vaporise a special non-toxic smoke fluid by propelling it over a heated element. A low-lying rolling *mist* can be obtained by lowering dry ice into boiling water. The resultant vapour is heavier than air and rolls across the stage floor. (Beware – dry ice burns flesh and must never be used without study of the manufacturer's recommendations for safe storage and usage.)

All types of smoke must be rehearsed and performed with particular care and sensitivity. Their action depends on so many factors, particularly atmospheric changes, that they can never be entirely predictable – a little too much can fill not just the

Smoke Generator
[*Rosco 1500*]

stage but the auditorium. An effect that was intended to help the production then succeeds in killing it off.

Bangs and Flashes

Although not really lighting effects, the electrics department is usually responsible for producing bangs, flashes, flares and pyrotechnic displays of all kinds. Meticulous attention to safety is essential in handling this sort of stuff, with particularly careful study of the manufacturer's instructions for each specific product. In particular, anyone handling a bomb tank or flash box should be able to see with their own eyes that the circuit is unplugged during the entire time that they are working on the device. Before plugging up, it is essential to check with a test lamp that the circuit is dead. Anyone firing a flash box should have sight of the device while firing.

Older type flash boxes are constructed of fire-proof materials and have terminals across which a piece of fuse-wire is used to ignite a plastic teaspoonful of the special powder. Newer types with a measured amount of powder pre-loaded in an enclosed capsule are much safer and more reliable. Bombs (often called *maroons*) are fired in special tanks with wire mesh coverings, and it is important to check that no one is near the tanks at firing time.

Modern flash systems use powder sealed in cartridges plugged into special pods fired from fail-safe control boxes with non-standard connections (*Le Maitre Pyroflash*)

Other Effects

Aerosols of cobwebs and melting snow are just some of the many assorted effects to be found in the catalogues. The 'confetti canon' which fires ½ kG of confetti on cue is dramatic, if limited in application, and there is even a soap bubble machine which must surely have a Shakespearean application if someone can hit upon the right production style to use the rainbow effects produced when light hits the bubbles.

Anything is possible so long as we remember that effects must be a positively integrated part of the production, not just a distracting decorative addition.

18
Comfort and confidence

Spotlights in ideal positions. Pointed precisely. Angles just right. Beams softly tuned. Colours delicately toned. Areas clearly selected. Atmosphere appropriate.

Enough? Not quite. There is another vital ingredient. The actor must feel comfortable and confident.

Lighting that is 'comfortable' to an actor is in fact rather in the nature of a controlled discomfort. Or perhaps 'professional discomfort' would be a more appropriate phrase. Actors need to feel a touch of glare in the eyes to believe that character can be projected. A sensitive actor feels the light: feels it enough to be aware of the degree of personal visibility, but not whether the balance between actors is correct. A sensitive actor who has studied lighting will develop an awareness of the sculptural quality of the light in the acting environment. (*Aside*: it is my sad personal observation that most acting schools teach less about the nature of design than most design schools teach about the nature of acting.)

Apart from sensing the eye light, actors may need some help in feeling comfortable. For example, in some auditoria, the foh lighting angles from ceiling bridges and side wall booms can be excellent in lighting design terms but leave a disconcerting black hole just where the audience is. Especially in comedy, there is little comfort in standing on a stage to embrace an audience void framed by a series of lighting arches (rather like goal posts) getting larger as they recede from the actor – a most disturbing inversion of the laws of perspective.

There is a possible solution that I have used with some success – although I have to measure that success by the cheerful uncomplaining disposition of my actors since any discussion with them might destroy the cheat (but honest cheat) upon which the method is based. As frequently observed in this book, horizontal lighting from the front of a low balcony is unsuitable as a component of normal actor lighting whether for visibility, sculpting or atmosphere. Well, at least from the audience viewpoint. But a little glow can be comforting to the actors. Fresnels on a flooded beam angle but with the top and bottom barndoors squashed to a slot and hitting straight in, no crossing, at eye level. A very small proportion of the total light. With 50 or 60 foh from top and sides bashing in with palest tints at about point 8, I have used half a dozen fresnels with middle saturation filters at about point $2\frac{1}{2}$.

A low intensity of light from this angle does practically nothing for the actor except induce a cosy comfort. With filtering, the technique can be used to encourage the actor to feel chilly misery but this is rarely required since sadness tends to be a more introverted emotion than joy. On the other hand, happiness and comedy are somewhat dependent on the actor receiving positive response of the kind that does not come from a void: eye-level light helps to provide an audience focus.

Actor comfort was an important function of footlights. They often gave more positive help to the actor in this way than their negative influence as a barrier between actor and audience.

In passing it should perhaps be noted that whereas light for drama exercises in schools is often used to create a working ambience for the actors (there is no audience), it is surprising that lighting is not used more often to create a working ambience for the actors in the workshop sessions that are now a regular part of the creative process in the rehearsal room. There seems to be some case for simple emotional lighting from time to time to stimulate the search for character. Once discovered, the character has to be projected by the actor's technical ways and means. At this point the lighting would become an aid for the audience rather than the actor. But I fantasise.

What is not fantasy is that the transfer from the rehearsal room to the stage is something of a traumatic experience for any actor. It is not easy to come to grips quickly with the projection demands of an auditorium, while acclimatising to a technological environment where various elements have to be integrated with each other and with the actors in what is often a ludicrously short time. This is where confidence is vital. The actors must have confidence in the lighting designer. Indeed the actors must have confidence in the whole production team. Perhaps in theory it might be enough for the actor to have confidence in the director who controls the whole production team. But increasingly complex technology and ever tougher schedules mean that the director just has to delegate large areas of responsibility in order to concentrate on the totality.

Lighting is a particularly important element in the confidence area: most other contributions produce designs in a graphic form which is understandable to the non-specialist. The performances can be seen growing in the rehearsal room and the set, costume and prop designs taking shape in the workshops. But the lighting design cannot be realised until a very late point in the production process.

Intensive planning is the main requirement to overcome this, but actor confidence is a vital adjunct. The actor must be able to accept from the lighting designer 'yes, we have a problem here, but we are working on it and the idea *will* work.' The main way to build confidence is naturally to ensure that at the next rehearsal all is right. But actor confidence must be sufficient to survive several interventions of Murphy's Rehearsal Law which states that unrelated disasters tend to occur to the same actor at the same cue daily.

Actor/lighting designer confidence can come in various ways. A little, inevitably, from reputation (but this has been known to work inversely!). Mutual confidence is easier in a company with regular actors and staff. Otherwise it is a matter of the lighting designer showing concern by frequent attendance at rehearsals. And talking to the actors informally from time to time – showing interest, knowledge and concern for the actor's problems. The actor is rightly worried by the mass of anonymous faces that can surround a production desk in an otherwise darkened auditorium – wearing 'cans' and chanting numbers. But if the faces are familiar and have shared a beer, a joke and a moan, the threat is diminished. It may be a much frayed cliché, but we need to repeat it daily: *theatre is a people industry*.

20
Light education

On the whole, I believe that careers in stage lighting are for those who might be described as 'theatre people who work in lighting' rather than 'lighting people who work in theatre'.

LIGHTING TECHNICIANS

A career as a theatre lighting technician is an ambition that is relatively straightforward to achieve, provided one has:

- Interest in, perhaps even a passion for, theatre.
- Determination to work in theatre lighting.
- Aptitude for adjusting and maintaining small-scale mechanical equipment.
- Aptitude for commonsense electrical and mechanical trouble-shooting.
- A sensitive eye.
- A sensitive ear.
- Physical stamina.
- Good head for heights.
- An acceptance of work patterns where hours are often long, irregular and unsocial, with periods of short intense pressure punctuated by long periods of standing by.

Until very recently, training for lighting crew, like most work in the theatre, was based on the informal apprenticeship basis of learning on the job. This traditional method is still possible, although a more formal approach is becoming increasingly common throughout the theatre industry. Several colleges offer courses which provide an introduction to theatre and its basic lighting and electrical theory and practice. There is often an element of secondment into theatres on a block or day-per-week basis. The electrical content of most of these courses is geared to elementary procedures for the maintenance and safe operation of stage lighting installations. Students who wish to prepare for a life in theatre electrics by studying in greater depth, particularly those with a strong aptitude for mathematics, may consider taking a non-theatre course in electrical

- And, if so, were we flexible enough in observing these changes and adapting our planned lighting?

How many problems were caused by the architecture of the venue?

- Could the foh lighting positions be improved?
- Or could we have made better use of the available positions?
- And did we always choose the best compromise when selecting hanging positions on stage?

Could the lights have been in better condition?

- Optically (dirty lenses or reflectors)?
- Mechanically?
- Electrically?

Did the focusing progress smoothly?

- With each light able to do its planned job?
- Or were there sometimes obstacles such as borders or flats in the way?
- And if so, should we have realised this in advance?

How was the plotting?

- Did the 'palette' of focused lights provide everything the director and the rest of the design team hoped for?
- And were we flexible enough in developing ideas rather than sticking too rigidly to our original concept?

How were our communications?

- Did the activities of the lighting team cause many surprises to each other and to the rest of the production team?

Were we on schedule?

- Or did we plan to try to do much in the time available?

Were we on budget?

- If not, where did we miscalculate?

19
Agenda for a postmortem

I always hope to learn by my mistakes – and by my successes, especially the unexpected ones. Ideally the team would sit down a couple of days after the opening night to pick over the bones of the production period. But usually everyone is too busy with the next show – or just wants to forget this one. For anyone who wants a postmortem, group or individual, I offer, as an agenda, my own checklist developed while looking out of the train window on the way home from thirty years of productions.

How well did the lighting serve the production?
- In aims?
- In the achievement of these aims?

Did we make good decisions about the style of lighting look?
- Did the lighting support the actors in interpreting the script and/or score?
- Could it have been more atmospheric?
- Or more selective?
- Was it too naturalistic?
- Or not naturalistic enough?
- Was it consistent throughout?

Did we get our priorities right?
- Or were there some brief lovely moments at the expense of the rest of the evening?

How good was our division of the stage into acting areas?
- Were there enough areas?
- Or too many?
- And did these areas conform to the actor movements?

And the division of the stage into colours?
- Did it provide the right mixing possibilities in the right places?

How close did the performance lighting match the ideas of the original discussions?
- Were the differences due to changes in ideas as the production developed in rehearsal?

or electronic engineering. This also offers career options beyond the somewhat precarious theatre industry.

Different job opportunities for members of theatre lighting crews (usually known as 'the electrics') offer alternative working patterns. Some people like the routine of producing theatres which present their own plays, others prefer working in a receiving theatre with a mixed programme of touring shows, while many opt for a freelance career. It is a matter of personal preference, linked to such considerations as temperament, family circumstances and job satisfaction.

In-service training courses are likely to become an increasing feature of theatre education. They offer a particularly effective way of building on experience and acquiring knowledge of new technologies and skills in handling and maintaining new equipment.

LIGHTING DESIGNERS

But how does one become a lighting designer? The traditional path has been a mixture of chance and persistence. While working in various areas of theatre, particularly in electrics or stage management and occasionally in set design, people discover an interest in light and an aptitude for handling it. Development as a lighting designer then becomes a process of persistence: first to be given design opportunities and then to learn from these opportunities. In the beginning there is a considerable element of chance. Particularly being in the right places at the right times to get opportunities to light shows – and particularly to do so in a sympathetic environment. But a major problem is that, whereas actors, musicians, set designers and costumiers can be auditioned, by the time a lighting designer's work is seen, it is usually too late to substitute an alternative. This encourages theatre managements to play safe in their choice of lighting designer and reduces opportunities for new people.

Chance and persistence are likely to remain major factors in career development but are becoming less of a normal way to get started. Although a proportion of actors, designers and technicians have always emerged by routes other than through the formal theatre educational system, and some will always continue to do so, the theatre industry is moving towards more structured methods of educating its personnel. Lighting design is no exception. Indeed there are several reasons why lighting design courses are an area of education particularly, even urgently, in need of development.

My generation of lighting designers grew up in parallel with the great technological surge of the last thirty years. We started to light with a small amount of simple equipment, gradually learning by on-the-job discovery as rigs grew in size and technological sophistication. The advances in technology were parallelled by a general desire of production teams to expand the contribution of light to the stage environment. Our aspirations had clear goals provided by Appia, Craig and the many others who had been frustrated by the technology and production attitudes of their time. With the art and the science becoming closely interactive and feeding each other as we juggled the desirable with the possible, the development pace was very quick. Today's young designers are faced with expectations of a higher lighting quality and more complex equipment options for achieving it. Although some problems have gone – particularly the limitations of the control boards of thirty years ago – new lighting designers have to take my generation's point of arrival as their point of departure. And so, before starting, they have to assimilate a considerable amount of the know-how that we acquired experimentally over a long period.

What personal qualities and aptitudes would seem desirable in a potential professional lighting designer? I would suggest:

- A committed interest in all aspects of theatre, and the performing and visual arts generally.
- A determination that puts being a lighting designer before financial security and a scheduled social life.
- A capacity for strongly imaginative visual thinking.
- An aptitude for absorbing the possibilities and limitations of various technologies, both new and old, for designing and managing lighting's contribution to staged performances.
- An ability to relate to, and work with, the other members of creative and interpretative teams.
- Verbal articulacy in asking, explaining and discussing.

I would not claim particularly high personal ratings on this list and I have omitted one particular aptitude which I lack and have regretted increasingly throughout my working life. And what is that? I wish I could draw. So much discussion about light has to be in verbal rather than visual terms. Light is so difficult to put into words that we are never sure if we mean the same thing: in my experience, we rarely do. I would love to be able to sketch alternatives while we talk. 'Do you mean this or that?' My ideal director would pick up a pencil and say 'well I rather see it like this'. Although scene designers have the ability, surprisingly few draw light. But how helpful it is when they do.

LIGHTING DESIGN COURSES

Working as part of a lighting team will always continue to be a learning situation, particularly observation of cause and effect. But how can we prepare people to benefit from this and provide them with a structured learning experience which will lead them gradually towards lighting public performances?

With the exception of the United States where lighting design is a well established major study in many university theatre departments, most of the world, including Britain, offers very few course opportunities for lighting design students. All stage management, technical and design courses contain lighting elements but there is no established tradition of specialised training for lighting designers. However, the position is changing. With courses like those in Hong Kong and Helsinki leading the way, lighting design education is on the march.

How should such courses be constructed? Is lighting design an appropriate specialist study to make before embarking on a professional career? Or should potential lighting designers begin with more general theatre studies and then return to college for specialist study after some experiences of working in theatre which would enable them to re-affirm, or even discover, lighting interests and aptitudes?

Perhaps lighting design education should be as flexible as possible, offering:

Foundation Lighting Design Courses

Essentially a pre-career-entry study, but also available in more concentrated form for those who already have considerable theatre experience and now wish to specialise in lighting. These courses would include:

- A wide introduction to theatre embracing its histories, philosophies, aspirations and achievements.
- An understanding of the processes of text analysis, direction and acting.
- A study of the workings and interrelationships of all the staging departments.
- An exploration of the fundamentals of lighting design.

Lighting Design Specialist Courses

Taken after a foundation course, with or without an intermediate period of professional work, these would be based as
far as possible on discovery with students placed in structured
situations offering an opportunity of discovering rather than receiving information. There would be:

- A major emphasis on lighting real productions under the
  supervision of experienced professional designers.

- A strong core of laboratory type projects devised to present
  opportunities for the lighting process to be explored in a
  wide range of alternative lighting styles with discovery
  based primarily on the relation of cause and effect.

- Considerable emphasis on team work, with students taking
  on the role of design leader in rotation.

- A gradual build-up in the complexity of projects, but including an occasional return to basics. Also occasionally working
  in styles favoured by the rest of a production team although
  contrary to the lighting designer's style.

- Theoretical studies in support of practical lighting, including script analysis with writers and directors, pictorial
  analysis with art historians, painters and sculptors and lighting history researched on the principle of to move forward,
  first look back.

The major problem of teaching lighting is the extensive
resources required. Although much can be done in a small
studio, access is required to stages of different form and size.
These resources need to be made available for considerable
periods of time. Multiply the time normally taken to rig and
light a production by the number of students involved. Even
without a margin added for experiment, it can be seen that a lot
of resource is taken up by a small number of students. Five or six
is not just the ideal size of a lighting group to allow everyone a
chance – it is virtually the maximum size to let everyone really
benefit. On this basis it would seem that really concentrated
specialist training in lighting design can only really be made
available to a very small number of people. This provides
another reason to suggest that studying lighting design in depth
should be a post-graduate and/or post-experience study for
those who have demonstrated aptitude, preferably in a working
theatre environment.

However, to return to the theme of the prologue to this
book, I firmly believe that all theatre education (including
acting) should include a considerable lighting content.

Further reading

LIGHTING
Richard Pilbrow: *Stage Lighting* (Cassell, London; Drama Book Specialists, New York)
Timothy Streader & John A. Williams: *Create Your Own Stage Lighting* (Bell)

DESIGN
Francis Reid: *Designing for the Theatre* (A & C Black, London; Routledge, New York)

STAGECRAFT & MANAGEMENT
Francis Reid: *The Staging Handbook* (A & C Black, London; Routledge, New York)
Francis Reid: *Theatre Administration* (A & C Black, London)

TECHNOLOGY
Donmar Reference Manual (Donmar, London)
George C. Izenour: *Theatre Technology* (McGraw Hill)

ARCHITECTURE
Roderick Ham: *Theatres – Planning Guidance for Design and Adaptation* (Architectural Press, London)
Richard Leacroft: *Theatre and Playhouse* (Methuen, London)

SOUND
Graham Walne: *Sound for the Theatre* (A & C Black, London; Routledge, New York)

UNDERSTANDING THE PLAYWRIGHT
Simon Gray: *An Unnatural Pursuit* (Faber & Faber, London)

UNDERSTANDING THE ACTOR
Peter Barkworth: *About Acting* (Secker & Warburg, London)
Simon Callow: *Being An Actor* (Methuen, London)
Alec Guiness: *Blessings in Disguise* (Hamish Hamilton, London)
Anthony Sher: *The Year of the King* (Chatto & Windus, London)

UNDERSTANDING THE DIRECTOR
Peter Brook: *The Shifting Point* (Methuen, London)
Jonathan Miller: *Subsequent Performances* (Faber & Faber, London)

PRODUCTION DIARIES
Stephen Fay: *The Ring – Anatomy of an Opera* (Secker & Warburg, London)
Jim Hiley: *Theatre at Work – The Diary of the National Theatre's Production of Brecht's Gallieo* (Routledge & Kegan Paul, London)

THEATRE HISTORY
James Roose-Evans: *Experimental Theatre from Stanislavsky to Peter Brook* (Routledge & Kegan Paul, London)
Glynne Wickham: *A History of the Theatre* (Phaidon, Oxford)

Glossary

A

Acting Area The area of the stage setting within which the actor performs. Also an obsolete type of fixed focus instrument used for downlighting.

Advance Bar A spot bar hung within the auditorium, close to the proscenium.

Apron Part of the stage projecting towards or into the auditorium. In proscenium theatres, the part of the stage in front of the main house curtain.

B

Backing Scenery behind a door, window, fireplace or similar opening. (Also the money invested in a commercial production.)

Backlight Light coming from behind scenery or actors to sculpt and separate them from their background.

Bar Horizontal metal tube of scaffolding diameter for hanging lights (*pipe* in North America).

Barndoor Four-shutter rotatable device which slides into the front runners of fresnel and PC focus spots to shape the beam and reduce stray scatter light.

Battens Lengths of overhead lighting floods arranged in 3 or 4 circuits for colour mixing. Also lengths of timber at the tops and bottoms of cloths.

Beam angle Angle of the cone of light produced by a spotlight.

Beamlight Lensless spotlight with parabolic reflector giving intense parallel beam.

Bifocal spot Profile spot with additional set of shutters to allow combination of hard and soft edges from the same instrument.

Black light UV (*q.v.*)

Bleed Lighting a scene behind a gauze to make the scene gradually visible through the gauze.

Board Contraction of *switchboard* or *dimmerboard*. The central control point for the stage lighting.

Boom Vertical pole, usually of scaffolding diameter, for mounting spotlights.

Boom arm Bracket for fixing spotlights to a boom.

Borders Neutral or designed strips of material hung above the stage to form a limit to the scene and mask the technical regions above the performance area.

Border lights North American term for battens (*q.v.*)

Brail To pull suspended scenery or lighting upstage or downstage from its natural free-hanging position by means of short rope lines attached to the ends of the fly bar.

Breast To pull suspended scenery or lighting upstage or downstage from its free hanging position by means of a rope line passed across the fly bar's suspension lines.

Bridge An access catwalk, passing over the stage or incorporated within the auditorium ceiling, usually to facilitate spotlight focusing. Also elevators which raise and sink sections of a stage floor.

Build (1) An increase in light intensity.
(2) To construct a scene from its component parts.

C

Channel A complete stage circuit (*q.v.*) including dimmer control.

Channel access The method (levers, pushes, keyboard, etc.) in a memory system by which individual channels are brought under operator control.

Chase To switch lights, usually electronically, in a looped sequence so that they appear to be 'chasing' each other.

Check Decrease in light intensity.

C.I.D. A type of high intensity discharge lamp, normally interchangeable with C.S.I. lamps but offering a light approximating more to daylight.

Circuit A complete path from the electrical supply to the light. When such a path includes a dimmer, it should be called a channel, but the word circuit is often used loosely to include channel.

Colour call A listing of all the colour filters required in each lighting instrument.

Colour temperature A method of measuring (in Kelvin units) the spectral content of 'white' light.

Colouvred Black coating baked on to the riser surfaces of a fresnel lens to reduce stray scatter light.

Control Surface Any device such as lever, push, wheel, rocker, mouse, pen, cursor, etc., used as an interface between an operator's fingers and a processing system which activates dimmers or motors controlling lighting instruments.

Cross-fade Lighting change where some of the channels increase in intensity while other channels decrease.

C.S.I. (*Compact Source Iodine*) A type of high intensity discharge lamp (cannot be dimmed electrically).

Cue The signal that initiates a change of any kind. *Lighting cue* is a change involving light intensity alterations.

Cyclorama Plain cloth extending around and above the stage to give a feeling of infinite space. Term is often rather loosely used for any blue skycloth, either straight or with a limited curve at the ends.

D

Dark A theatre temporarily or permanently closed to the public.

Dead (1) The plotted height of a piece of suspended scenery or bar of lights (*trim* in America).
(2) Discarded items of scenery.

Dichroic Colour filters which work by reflecting unwanted parts of the spectrum rather than absorbing them in the manner of traditional filters.

Diffuser A filter, often called a *frost*, which softens a light beam, particularly its edge.

Dimmer Device which controls the amount of electricity passed to a light and therefore the intensity of that light's brightness.

Dips Small traps in the stage floor giving access to electrical sockets (*floor pockets* in North America).

Directional diffuser A filter which not only softens the beam but spreads it along a chosen axis.

Director Has the ultimate responsibility for the interpretation of the script through control of the actors and supporting production team.

Discharge lamps Special high powered light sources whose use is normally restricted to follow spots and projection because of difficulties in remote dimming by electrical means.

Downstage   The part of the stage nearest to the audience.

E

Ellipsoidal   Strictly a type of reflector used in many profile spots but extended in North America to cover all profile spots.

F

False Proscenium   A portal (*q.v.*), particularly one in the downstage area.

Flash out   Checking whether lights are working by switching them on one at a time.

Floats   Jargon for footlights.

Flood   Simple instrument giving fixed spread of light.

Flys   Area above the stage into which scenery can be lifted out of sight of the audience.

Focusing   Strictly speaking, the adjustment of lights to give a clearly defined image; but usually used to cover the whole process of adjusting the direction and beam of spotlights in which the desired image may be anything but clearly defined.

FOH   All instruments which are 'front of house', i.e. on the audience side of the proscenium.

Follow spot   Spotlight with which an operator follows actors around the stage.

Footlights   Long strips of flooding equipment along the front of the stage arranged in 3 or 4 circuits for colour mixing.

Fresnel spot   Spotlight with soft edges due to fresnel lens which has a stepped moulding on the front and a textured surface on the back.

Frost   A diffuser filter used to soften a light beam.

FUF   Full-up-finish. An increase to bright light over the last couple of bars of a musical number.

Fuse   Protective device, either cartridge or piece of special wire, which melts when rated electrical current is exceeded.

G

Gate   The optical centre of a profile spot where the shutters are positioned and where an iris or gobo can be inserted.

Gauze   Fabric which becomes transparent or solid under appropriate lighting conditions (*Scrim* in North America).

Gobo   A mask placed in the gate (*q.v.*) of a profile spotlight for simple outline projection. Also used, with softened focus, to texture the beam.

Grid   The arrangement of wooden or metal slats above which are mounted the pulley blocks of the flying system.

Groundrow   A low piece of scenery standing on the stage floor. Also lengths of lighting placed on the stage floor.

Group   A subdivision, temporary or permanent, of the channels in a control system.

H

HMI   A type of high intensity discharge lamp used mainly in scenic projection and follow spots (cannot be dimmed electrically).

Hook clamp   A clamp for fixing an instrument to a horizontal bar, usually of scaffolding diameter.

Houselights   The decorative lighting in the auditorium.

I

Instrument   A stage lighting unit, such as a spotlight or flood. An American term but coming into increasing international use. See also *lantern* and *luminaire*.

Iris An adjustable circular diaphragm to alter the gate size in a profile spot. Also the muscle-operated diaphragm in the human eye which adjusts the eye's aperture to changing light intensities.

Isora A plastic skycloth, lit from behind.

K

Kilowatt See *Wattage*

L

Ladder Framework in the shape of a ladder (but not climbable) for hanging side lighting.

Lamps The light source within an instrument, but sometimes used as an alternative to the word instrument.

Lantern A luminaire (*q.v.*) designed or adapted for stage use. A traditional word now being overtaken by 'instrument'.

Leko North American term for a type of ellipsoidal profile spot. Use often extended to all makes of ellipsoidal.

Limes Jargon for follow spots and their operators.

Linear flood A flood using a long thin double-ended halogen lamp, allowing the reflector to be designed for an increased beam spread.

Load The lights controlled by an individual dimmer and limited by the rating of that dimmer.

Luminaire The international word for any lighting instrument of any kind (not just the specialised lighting instruments used in the theatre).

M

Magic Sheets Originally a simplified light plan for quick reference, but increasingly a control surface (*q.v.*) providing direct channel access by touching symbols on a plan.

Marking Placing small discreet marks on the stage floor (temporarily with tape, more permanently with paint) to aid the positioning of scenery and props during a change.

Masking Neutral material or scenery which defines the performance area and conceals the technical areas.

Master A lever or push which overrides (or 'masters') a complete preset, or group within a preset or selected memory.

Memory Lighting control systems where channel intensities for each cue are filed automatically in an electronic store.

Multiplexing Passing control instructions, particularly to dimmers or remotely focusable lights, by sending all information in digital format along a single pair of screened wires.

O

O.P. 'Opposite prompt' side of the stage – stage right, i.e. actor's right when facing the audience.

P

Palette The range of individual light beams prepared for mixing to 'paint' the stage picture.

Pan Horizontal (left/right) movement of an instrument.

Parcan The simple instrument which holds a par lamp and therefore does not require any optical system of lenses or reflectors.

Par lamp A sealed beam lamp with the filament contained within the same glass envelope as an optical system producing a near parallel beam.

Patching A sort of central 'telephone exchange' where dimmers can be connected to appropriate socket outlets.

PC   see *Plano convex* and *Prism convex*.

Pebble   see *Prism convex lens*.

Perches   Lighting positions (often on platforms) at each side of the stage, immediately behind the proscenium.

Pilots   Low intensity or blue lights around the sides of the stage which do not illuminate the acting area but allow the actors to move about safely. See also *working lights*.

Pin matrix   A method of selecting control channels into groups by inserting pins into the holes of a matrix where one coordinate represents channels, and the other coordinate represents group masters.

Pipe   North American term for bar (*q.v.*).

Pipe ends   Spotlights on the ends of lighting bars, crosslighting to model dancer's bodies.

Plano convex lens   A lens with one flat surface and one curved surface. This 'PC' lens and the fresnel lens are the alternatives normally used in spotlights.

Playback   The part of a memory system where memorised lighting states are recalled to control the light on stage via master levers or pushes.

Portal   Framed masking border bolted to framed masking legs, often given decorative treatment.

Practical   Light fitting which is not merely decorative but is wired to light up. Also used for any prop which works.

Prefocus cap   A special lamp base which ensures that the filament lines up precisely with the optics of a spotlight.

Preset   Anything which is positioned in advance of its being required – such as props placed on the stage before the performance. A control system where each channel has more than one lever to allow intensity levels to be set (i.e. *preset*) in advance of a cue.

Prism convex lens   A PC lens incorporating some diffusion in its structure. Also known as *pebble convex*.

Profile Spot   A spotlight which projects the outline (i.e. the *profile*) of any chosen shape and with any desired degree of hardness/softness (in North America often called *ellipsoidal* or *leko*).

Profiled Cue   A lighting change where the rates of increasing and decreasing intensities accelerate or decelerate during the progress of the change.

Proscenium Theatre   The traditional form of theatre where the audience sit in a single block facing the stage, with a fairly definite division between audience and stage. The position of this division is known as the *proscenium* and takes many forms from a definite arch, not unlike a picture frame, to an unstressed termination of auditorium walls and ceiling.

P.S.   'Prompt side' of the stage – stage left, i.e. actor's left when facing the audience.

Pyrotechnics   Bombs, bangs, flashes etc., usually fired electrically.

R

Rating   The maximum and minimum power in kilowatts that can be controlled by a circuit or dimmer channel.

Record   Plotting a cue state by filing it in the electronic data storage of a memory board.

Resistance dimmer   An older mechanical form of dimmer which reduces the flow of electrical current to a light by progressively converting the surplus into heat.

Rigger's control   A remote portable hand-held control unit which allows channels or groups to be switched from the stage for focusing when the control room is unmanned.

Rim light   Backlighting which creates a

'rim' of light around the actors to separate them from their background.

Rock boards Control boards with particularly flexible facilities for 'playing' channels or groups and for setting up complex sequences for flashing and chasing.

S

Saturation rig A type of lighting installation in a repertoire theatre where the maximum number of spotlights are rigged in every available position.

Scatter Low intensity light cast outside the main beam of an instrument.

Screw cap A simple lamp base, used only for battens, floods and older spotlight types. See *Prefocus*.

Scrim North American term for *gauze* (*q.v.*)

Scrollers Colour changer where a roll of filters are taped together and positioned by a very fast motor activated by digital signals from a control system which includes a memory facility.

Shin Busters Low level lights at stage floor level, used mainly for dance.

Sightlines Lines drawn on plan and section to indicate limits of audience vision from extreme seats, including side seats, front and back rows, and seats in galleries.

Silks Diffusion filters which stretch the light in a chosen direction.

Slots Side lighting positions incorporated within auditorium walls.

Soft Patch An electronic facility within a control system to allow dimmers to be allocated to channels as required.

Solid state A situation, particularly in intensity control, where all action is carried out electronically without moving parts.

Spigot An adapter screwed to the hanging bolt of an instrument to enable it to be mounted on a floor stand.

Spill Stray or scatter light outside the main beam.

Spotlight An instrument giving control of the angle of the emerging light beam and therefore of the size of area lit.

Spot line A temporary line dropped from the grid to suspend something in an exact special position.

Standing Scenery ('standing set') or lights ('standing light') which does not change during the performance.

Strobe Device giving a fast series of very short light flashes under which action appears to be frozen.

T

Theatre-in-the-Round A form of staging where the audience totally encircle the acting area.

Throw Distance between a light and the actor or object being lit.

Thrust Form of stage which projects into the auditorium so that the audience are seated on at least two sides.

Thyristor Electronic device which chops the wavelength of an alternating current and has become the standard dimmer.

Tilt Vertical (up/down) movement of an instrument.

Transformation An instant scene change, often effected by exploiting the varying transparency of gauze under different lighting conditions.

Trim North American term for the height above stage level of a hanging piece of scenery, lights or masking (the equivalent in Britain is one of the meanings of *dead*).

Tripe Several cables from a lighting bar taped together from the end of the bar until the position where they are plugged into the socket outlets of the permanent wiring installation.

Truss A framework of alloy bars and triangular cross-bracing (all of scaffolding diameter) providing a rigid structure, particularly useful for hanging lights.

Tungsten lamps Older type of lamps (the stage types are high wattage versions of standard domestic lamps) whose tungsten filaments gradually lose the brightness of their light output.

Tungsten halogen lamps Newer lamps (now virtually standard in professional theatre) which maintain their initial brightness of light output throughout life.

U

Upstage The part of the stage furthest from the audience.

UV Ultra violet light (from which harmful radiations have been filtered out) used to light specially treated materials which fluoresce in an otherwise blackened stage.

V

Variable beam profile Profile spotlight using a type of zoom (*q.v.*) arrangement where the differential movement of two lenses allows wide variations in both beam size and quality.

VDU (Visual Display Unit) A television type monitor screen in which all the information stored in a memory system can be displayed, including the changing channel levels during a cue and the channel levels filed in any memory.

W

Wattage The power of consumption of a lamp, or the maximum available power from a dimmer. A kilowatt is 1,000 watts.

Ways The number of channels in a control system.

Wings The technical areas to the sides of the acting area. Also, scenery standing where the acting area joins these technical areas.

Working lights Stage lights independent of the main production lighting system. Switched from the prompt corner, but sometimes with an overriding switch in the control room.

Z

Zoom A differential movement of two lenses in an optical system. In a simple zoom, the lenses are moved independently, but in more complex forms a single movement alters the size of the beam while the image remains in constant focus. Used in advanced profile spots and scene projectors.

Index

All numbers in *italics* refer to glossary.